TROUBLES SWAPPED FOR SOMETHING FRESH

TROUBLES SWAPPED FOR SOMETHING FRESH

MANIFESTOS AND UNMANIFESTOS

EDITED BY RUPERT LOYDELL

SALT

CAMBRIDGE

PUBLISHED BY SALT PUBLISHING
Fourth Floor, 2 Tavistock Place, Bloomsbury, London WC1H 9RA United Kingdom

Selection and foreword © Rupert Loydell, 2009
Individual contributions © the contributors, 2009

The right of Rupert Loydell to be identified as the
editor of this work has been asserted by him in accordance
with Section 77 of the Copyright, Designs and Patents Act 1988.

Salt Publishing 2009
Reprinted with corrections 2009

Printed and bound in the United Kingdom by Lightning Source UK

Typeset in Swift 9.5 / 13

ISBN 978 1 84471 471 1 paperback

1 3 5 7 9 8 6 4 2

CONTENTS

CONTENTS

CONTENTS

viii

CONTENTS

FOREWORD

1. I have always hated manifestos.

2. I am editing an anthology with the working title of *Manifesto!* for Salt.

3. I offered.

4. I would prefer new, unpublished work, but will also consider previously published work.

5. I am looking for poetry, poetics and poetical manifestos, in the form of poetry or [poetic?] texts rather than critical articles or essays, but also hope for work which will blur the boundaries. I am looking for a diversity of opinion, attitude, approaches and styles: the aim is to aid and start discussion, not to offer a single argument or position.

6. Manifestos as ideas to respond to and challenge. Questionable polemic.

7. With some wit involved.

8. I really do need this work as soon as possible.

9. It is important to think. Language does not speak itself.

10. Forward!

RUPERT LOYDELL

TROUBLES
SWAPPED FOR
SOMETHING
FRESH

NINE WAYS OF LOOKING AT
A MANIFESTO

1. It's not as if
    not so long ago
    language was not so.

2. 'This baboon teaches letters.'
    Tell me, Thoth,
    what this says about baboons.
    And what does it say about letters?

3. A morning hymn to
    A sixfold paronomasic
    As the sun of a new day.

4. 'Since it is a map of anything
    Since it is the total description
    Since they banned the bon mot' &c.

5. Anonymous led from the start.
    Analysis came last.

6. He's listed all the things
    he only thinks of finally
    but there is no natural word order.
    Before transmutation
    no document's a poem.

7. All we know is this particular
    planet's being hung out to dry.
    Any day I will wake up
    speaking a language not dead but
    subject to recent legislation.

8. An emblem once put it like this:
    omen, ornament or name.
    Another said:
    presence, person or response.

9. A trap part art. Vague
    i.e. undefined
    but I know which verge it's under.
    Find me its apples.
    Wait for the applause.

ALAN HALSEY

POETIC DISSONANCE: A MANIFESTO

ANDREA MOORHEAD

1.

attitudes bumping against logic, tree trunks still straight after all the wind last night, words cascading down the side of the house, snow or ice pellets who can tell, the grammar of expression follows its own course, riles adjective and verb the flesh seeking something other than this concrete casing, this stepping around at midnight with heavy wings drooping by the door, a wax repair sets in motion other winds, ice still knocking against the windows, the temperature holding steady at freezing, this cannot indicate a major storm, but the arteries are wild tonight and the face still wrapped in stone or is it really wool shed by a thousand clouds., the path to logic has many stones, colored and ripped out of context, the waves roll onto the sand, whatever happened to the last passage to the clipped part recording your voice, or was it really only the only of ice drumming down the house, working out the seams, letting in moonlight or the salt cracked stain of waves sheltered close to the heart?

2.

bones are manifest as ice is manifest as the rolling sound of your heart is manifest but the grammar pulls against the ribs rolls over bone and sinew can't you see the night here can't you smell the sea seeping into the inner cavities, can't you remember what we did together where we went whom we saw the sight of a lion on the far horizon or was it an antelope you say an antelope I feel the night sky is punctured, your words scrambled again, my ears are plugged up with molten wax with the lava-pressed too hard against the back door a volcano you say an eruption of the earth you say that too loudly all night long can't you admit that the sun has been crushed to these smoldering embers in your hands burning again as we try to rise and leave this place worry and resettle the weight of flesh on fire.

3.

seeds don't take up any room, they're dry and light, round or pointed, nasturtium and morning glory the fragrant lift of cosmos or marigold, my hands are stained with the wind rustling the leaves all night, putting down under the water a fragrance we can still hear haunting and the bodies are calm today, lifting up the seeds to the light, they don't take up any room, do they, and their scent has a pull we cannot deny.

4.

no body a light the source left trembling even if water has flowed around the trunk settled down by the base of the apple something haunts the mind now some kind of sound pulling out the earth moving the trembling to one side, lifting the tense of burning light the slow soft wandering of the tongue when the night wind is cool and the mind burrowed deep under, no body a light the source and we can still perceive the dim outline on the horizon, something smoldering under the rain, something fragrant pungent lavender edged and pure while the words cascade down all during the morning leaving a trace of the night wind and the sudden apprehension of something burning at peace.

ANDREA MOORHEAD

A POETICS OF ABSENCE

ANDREW TAYLOR

At night I think of you, I haven't forgotten.
Is blossom memorial enough?

There is a need for change, I feel that need
self-definition is the hardest part

At the moment of crisis, phones shift
from being mere tools of convenience.
They begin to create a poetry of unease.[1]

Is this a poetry of unease?

The excitement is in producing the unknown.
The city seduces
     the proximity of memory

Communication with oneself is essential

The field of the poet's experience was democratized
to a degree that levelled it to one enormous field of
closely observed particulars—both physical and mental—[2]

The present is being eaten by the past
belief and proximity are connected closely

From the heart
     despite cliché
          a fear of drowning

Poetics steals from anywhere [3]

A distracted geography
        home from distance
you were so beautiful

from 'Catalf':[4]

        Gone my friend   grief will make her heart burst

        Can we go on like this with our hearts tied to the land?[5]

        There is no comfort in this world that's why I love you today[6]

        Must you be on your way?

There are too many ghosts of the past in my life living with me[7]

Communication the everyday
broken soul loss heartache
no desire to win competitions

a discourse of the normal with clarity
reader's desire poet's intention

creation and interpretation
dialogue with myself
irrelevance of intention

The canvas spotted with paint and glitter: *It was a bad painting and it's getting better*
Memory is key no matter how old or recent

Loss is key

ANDREW TAYLOR

from 'Poetry and Skin Cream': [8]

> When the fog lifts and you walk away
> I hope that you'll glance over your shoulder
> and wave from the built up distance

from 'Catalf': [9]

> Things will never be the same
> again light will angle differently
> cold will eat summer

How things will be after event
how things will sit

Come to me once more my love [10]

A sense of passing with hope

Writing the self the self is writing

If I knew there was any other way to you
I'd walk sand and miles any other way get close to you
and everything I have to say has probably been said many better ways
Sometimes I have you in my head and loving with you I am happy
I think of things to say to you of evenings we spent in another place
I sit alone and take care of my head all the feelings that I have in front of me
Changes that we could have made all the things we could have done together [11]

The commonality of language. A woman in Chile, and a man
in Manhattan can read poetry from Liverpool [12]

Is the ultimate poetry created out of personal pain?

Writing is a way to trace hunger and hunger is nothing if not a void [13]

Is this a poetry of experience? One of personal anguish?

Join images as they are joined in the mind: only thus can two images connect like wires and
spark [14]

Buildings absorb memories they are stored
upon return these memories come alive

Photographs recharge bring closer to mind events
After a death it is common practice to gather photographs

'You Should Gather the Photographs Together': [15]

> Back to her streets and familiarity: 1950s Gladys,
> Ocean Fleets, buildings in need of smog damaged
> sand blast.
>
> Camels on the Mersey. Elephants at Lime Street.
>
> Hanker for past. A purer city. Billboards painted
> on walls: 'Phillips and Charles' viewed from Costa's
> first floor window.

ANDREW TAYLOR

In parkland near Port Sunlight, a fallen tree is chopped
ready for firewood.

She consumes me, desire to return to her welcoming arms.

Events imagined or real events as told?
It's odd that I can walk streets
that my Aunty walked when she was young
Do her memories interfere with mine? The city is never far from mind

Objects become muses of memory [16]

The creation of the unknown
Do dreams seep into walls?
The morning chimney light
proof of existence
        Do you remember mornings shared?
Do you understand my language?

Is it about communication or the ability to communicate? [17]

We are born into language but a language not our own [18]

Through acquisition we share
a common language
shared words shared meaning

A walk leads to sadness back to
a garden and

Summer's Arc of Sun: [19]

> Red brick lit from light summer's arc—of sun
> rook sat on chimney stack
> peaceful gaze shattered by swallow's
> fighter plane attack, rook shifts

he played amongst the lavender
like velvet to be coaxed
I catch the essence
that lingers

How I wish you were here with me now [20]

It is in the lines [. . .] it is in the coldness of Cathedrals [21]

The power to create the power to invent

Technique over content content over technique
poets are writing machines

Be open to the poem's approach
let it wash over you sense its inspiration

An active compliance the poem is the poem

Accept the lineage

One of the limits of inspiration may be its very spontaneity [23]

ANDREW TAYLOR

Revisiting may be painful but productive

words appear different upon reflection
The authenticity is in the spontaneity—the spark of an idea
and the generative notion of poetics

the poetics of pain

4 Real

Dust settles on papers stacked
Poems are understood when they are achieved [24]

Mourning works a terrible logic. It is a monster, like Time, and akin to Death — perhaps a younger sibling — that devours and rebuilds only to devour again. For that, it is like poetry as well. Poetry is itself another monster, a murmur, as some philosophers would have it, between worlds, if not between the living and the dead, than between the possibilities of each [25]

Perhaps it is anticipation
like journeys along the Welsh coast

A poetics of absence

where clouds form patterns on grass

Can the reader share in the experience?

A remnant of a mark on the forearm
a reminder

like not washing the towel like sitting alone

on the stairs like putting the red wrap on the bed
as a reminder

Do these words detach at birth and go about the world without control?

Poem as artefact as poetics

How quickly the dead are gone into us, sealed away into their only after-life, the one of our memory, the echo of laughter shared, the quiet bonds and history of friendship that slips discreetly beyond life and death

like realising this is permanent

from 'Conker': [27]

> The trees are losing their leaves
>
> That goodness via tablet form
> runs through those scarred veins
> pumped slow
>
> The tarmac catches the afternoon light
>
> Three movements to fade
> a handshake a kiss a wave
> fades to white

ANDREW TAYLOR

You were my absence.
Wherever I breathed, you found me
lying in the word
that spoke its way back
to this place [28]

Connect through text
inconceivable to be without
such facility

futility in understanding
two worlds collide
the before the after

Build a soundtrack
artefacts possessions
what was yours is now mine

the authority of authorship

poetry should be written any way it chooses

Sadness and joy are never separate [29]

Early morning
and late at night
the spirit of silence

before the hidden track

Contemplation during
creative lull

Is poetry love's labour?

I believe that poetry is an action, ephemeral or solemn, in which there enter as equal partners solitude and solidarity, emotion and action, the nearness to oneself, the nearness to mankind and to the secret manifestations of nature [30]

Poetics is ethical—it is worded beyond a man's lifetime [31]

to be inhabited
and understood

gathered as memento

the sound of an ice-cream
van merges with birdsong
another era an interval
given to history

Afternoon spent passing
shared finality
evening away lost to time

padding to quietness
reminder behind
left amongst the everyday

ANDREW TAYLOR

routine uninterrupted
shaped by presence and absence

Remembering brings the emptiness, the acutely painful awareness of irreparable loss. [32]

from 'How Animals Work': [33]

      this nature of happiness
      an extension of adequacy

      tolerable and bearable
      search the heart of the other

Every time I see the grave, I get that empty feeling where something was, and isn't anymore, and it will never be again. [34]

Writing a new desk a new
location a new approach

of difficulty
blinds study of landscape

this letter of mourning
an undisclosed recipient

'spots of time' [35]

The city seduces still
    the proximity of memory

A plot of permanence
mosaic of memories

you remain

I cannot forget

NOTES

1 Iain Sinclair, *Theatre of the City* in *The Guardian*, Thursday July 14th 2005, (London and Manchester).

2 Siri Hustvedt, *What I Loved* (London: Sceptre, 2003), p.177.

3 Robert Sheppard, *The Necessity of Poetics*, (Liverpool: Ship of Fools, 2002), p.5.

4 Andrew Taylor 'Catalf' *And the Weary are at Rest*, (Sunnyoutside Press, 2008).

5 Epic45, 'Walk led to Happiness' on *England Fallen Over EP* (Make Mine Music: MMM014, 2005).

6 Epic45, 'The Year Ahead' on *England Fallen Over EP* (Make Mine Music: MMM014, 2005).

7 Portal, 'Waves & Echoes' on *Waves and Echoes* (Make Mine Music: MMM012 2005).

8 Andrew Taylor, 'Poetry and Skin Cream' in *Poetry and Skin Cream* (Liverpool: erbacce Press, 2004), p.1.

9 Andrew Taylor 'Catalf' *And the Weary are at Rest*, (Sunnyoutside Press, 2008).

10 Mark Kozelek, 'Duk Koo Kim' (Vinyl Films 10″ vinyl recording 2004).

11 Julian Cope, 'Torpedo', *Fried* (Mercury Records 1984).

12 Due to having my own website, {www.andrewtaylorpoetry.com} where I can post poems, usually work which has been previously published in magazines and books, I have received communications from people in places such as New York City and Chile.

13 Siri Hustvedt, *What I Loved* (Sceptre: London, 2003), p.365.

14 Allen Ginsberg, *What Book: Buddha Poems From Beat To Hiphop*, (ed. Gary Gach) (Berkeley: Parallax Press: 1998), quoted at http://www.poetspath.com/transmissions/messages/ginsberg.html 10th August 2005.

ANDREW TAYLOR

15 Andrew Taylor, 'You Should Gather the Photographs Together' published in *Aesthetica Magazine* # 5 April 2004.

16 Siri Hustvedt, *What I Loved* (Sceptre: London, 2003), p.364.

17 This question highlights the difficulty which arises when the question is asked why people chose to write poetry.

18 Gregory Betts, *Plunderverse: A Cartographic Manifesto*, summer 2005 www.poetics.ca # 5 An Open Site for Dialogue on Poetic Theory and Practice, 10th August 2005 www.poetspath.com (http://www.poetics.ca/poetics05/05betts.html).

19 Andrew Taylor, 'Summer's Arc of Sun', unpublished poem, 20th July 2005.

20 New Order, 'In a Lonely Place' (Factory Records, FAC33, 1981).

21 Andrew Taylor, 'It Is In The Lines' unpublished poem, 3rd May 2005.

22 This refers to Les Murray's quote referring to the creation of a poem: 'Sometimes it starts without your knowing that you're getting there, and it builds in your mind like a pressure. I once described it as being like a painless headache, and you know there's a poem in there, but you have to wait until the words form.' Undated, www.lesmurray.org , 17th March 2001.

23 Stephen Brockwell *Spontaneous Speech Maps: A Discussion on Poetics* June 2003 www.poetics.ca # 2 ISSN 1703–9029 An Open Site for Dialogue on Poetic Theory and Practice, 10th August 2005 (http://www.poetics.ca/poetics02/02norris.html).

24 By this I refer to the completion of the poem to the satisfaction of the poet.

25 Michael Brennan, *In absentia: Mourning and Friendship* April 2005 www.jacketmagazine.com Jacket 27 April 2005 (http://jacketmagazine.com/27/breninabsent.html) 14th August 2005

26 Ibid.

27 Andrew Taylor 'Conker' *And the Weary are at Rest*, (Sunnyoutside Press, 2008).

28 Paul Auster from 'Ecliptic.Les Halles' in *Ground Work: Selected Poems and Essays 1970–1979* (London: Faber and Faber, 1991), p. 38.

29 Michael Ford, e-mail to author dated 4th August 2005.

30 Pablo Neruda, from *Nobel Lectures, Literature 1968–1980*, *Editor-in-Charge* Tore Frängsmyr, Editor Sture Allén, (Singapore: World Scientific Publishing Co., 1993) quoted at, undated, www.poetspath.com July 29th 2005 (http://www.poetspath.com/transmissions/messages/Pablo_neruda_lect.html)

31 Mathieu Brosseau, at www.mathieubrosseau.com 2005, undated, August 25th 2005 (http://poetique.mathieubrosseau.com/tosee2.html)

32 William Burroughs, *Cabin on the Lake* in *Word Virus The William Burroughs Reader* eds., James Grauerholz and Ira Silverberg (London: Flamingo, 1999), p. 525.

33 Andrew Taylor 'How Animals Work' published in *Ditch*, 2008.

ANDREW TAYLOR

34 William Burroughs, *Cabin on the Lake* in *Word Virus The William Burroughs Reader* eds., James Grauerholz and Ira Silverberg (London: Flamingo 1999) p. 525.

35 William Wordsworth, *The Prelude, Book XI Imagination and Taste How Impaired and Restored*, (London: Oxford University Press 1960), p. 213 line 208.

POETRY

ANDY BROWN

Poetry reaches here and there by soaring. It points in the wrong direction and heads off there regardless; it directs us to the ossuary, to museum drawers in bloom, to birds and the green facts of nesting.

Poetry is the lesson of the doubtful person, pausing. It is implicit in the life of an expert on things and an authority on nothing. Poetry is a series of controlled blunders.

Poetry is living elsewhere; the city radiant with all of its ideas; the open throat of days we inhabit with abandon. Poetry is an outhouse in the woods where our story begins, surrounded by the rhythmic ratchets of frogs.

Poetry dances with happiness at the start of the new feast. It is the second spring of our tango across the tundra.

Poetry is Ice Age Man in the cave of himself, making effigies of beasts and killing them before he goes out on the real hunt with the magic of that killing on his side. Poetry is the migration of a herd of animal statues.

Poetry is troubles swapped for something fresh; the monstrance containing the host. The dead, the beloved, the detested—these are some of its objects.

Poetry is change; a chord the tension snaps. The poet reveals a trap for forms of magic.

Poetry stills to a lagoon at low tide. Its dredge hauls yield a final treat we share.

Poetry—the upturned saw blade of its kiss; its crucial first cut.

SECOND SILENT MANIFESTO

I don't know. I don't know. I don't know. I don't know. I don't know. I don't know. I don't know where to begin. I don't like the confidence apparently assumed in most written statements. Of only one thing I am quite sure. I don't know.

Don't answer. Please don't tell me. Don't say. Not where to begin—where not to begin. Only sanctuary—but where is sanctuary? Sanctuary is in a book—so I write books. But there is nothing to say—certainly there is nothing to say in 'writing' that most general of all contexts.

Oracular pretension of writing. Smug assumption of the interest and attention of others. A secret space of wondering, wandering. Formalized exactitude of nothingness. Poetic expansion of the empty, waiting silence.

Declaration of independence, but independence from what? First of all, from the siren song of conversation. Reinvention of the monologue, of the basics, of the essentials. Construction of a world from the beginning, but each subtle defining eliminating a multitude of other possible universes. Besides, this writing only occurred because this table where I brought my coffee happened to have a piece of paper on it. So, you dear hypnotized, belabored reader pre-seduced into spending priceless moments of your life on someone else's aimless mumbling.

I don't know, yes, but this is not to say I don't care. You probably won't believe this, while easily accepting many of my other assertions. Possibly all of them.

NICK PIOMBINO

HOW TO CAPTURE A POEM

ANGELA TOPPING

Look for one at midnight
on the dark side of a backlit angel
or in the space between a sigh
and a word. Winter trees, those
elegant ladies dressed in diamonds
and white fur, may hide another.

Look for the rhythm in the feet
of a waltzing couple one, two, three-ing
in an empty hall, or in the sound
of any heartbeat, the breath of a sleeper,
the bossy rattle of keyboards in offices,
the skittering of paper blown along.

You could find a whole line
incised into stone or scrawled on sky.
Words float on air in buses, are bandied
on street corners, overheard in pubs,
caught in the pages of books, sealed
behind tight lips, marshalled as weapons.

Supposing you can catch a poem,
it won't tell you all it knows. Its voice
is a whisper through a wall, a streak of silk
going by, the scratch of a ghost, the creaks
of a house at night, the sound of the earth
vibrating in spring, with all its secret life.

You have to listen: the poem chooses itself,
takes shape and begins to declare what it
        is.
Honour the given, else it will become
        petulant.

When you have done your best,
you have to let it go. Season it with salt
from your body, grease it with oil from
        your skin.

Release it. It has nothing more to do
with you. You're no more its owner
than you hold the wind. Never expect
        gratitude.

MY WHOLE LIFE THAT I KNOW OF,
I'VE BEEN LIVING: A TRIPTYCH

SINCERITY IRONY MILKSHAKE

Bring back sincerity milkshakes.
This is the perfect irony of example
for statement's sake. That I can no longer function
devalues Umberto Eco. I don't think it's so much
that defiance resolved to hope
as I've got this really HUGE-ASS issue
with fakery, my own foremost
among the kids' shows. I'm aware of the irony
that comedy markets a milkshake
that tastes like meat, but really, do you know
what soy cows say? How things
can be flipped on their head
becomes a toxic substance when you sit around
mixing your Buddhist irony and straightfoward
Country and Western pop craft, as if this
is a riddle commune afterall.
It's like icing on the cake, isn't it,
the icing on the cake? Like strawberries
in a yummy sincerity of finesse
and complex postmodern infatuations
with the liquid crack of irony. Where do we go,
Buttonhole, if you have nothing to hold?
After writing this and getting wrought
with painful and deadpan distortions
of soul, I like to watch speedbumps, I mean,
really, digging the riverbed for solid gold
radiates its own kind of benighted 'rah.'
Good luck. I mean that with no wink
in the syllables.

BOB HICOK

IDEOLOGY POETRY KITES

Mohamed has related poetry to life by saying
that sane resists totalitarian aesthetics.
Discourse events and other parts of balance
between two kites and ideology, how beautifully
that scenery flies up to the sky
from the small boy's hand. For those few readers
unfamiliar with moving across Cloudland,
she rides her bike, eschewing 'the diamond absolutes.'
Believe me when I say all scavenging by dogs,
bats and kites, a person guiding it, dives
as much as wind, resists a description
of evening birds. Magma describes the poet
flying kites on her idea of image. This new
verbose assortment, some wide variety of issues
have been rhetoric. The ideology in defense
of top-spinning, personal and creative,
from his mistress's indisposition, is again
a cancionero of anti-war science and Judaism.
No triumph anathema to you and me! Not in spring,
the autobiographical sequence near Tallapiedra
stopping to watch the seashore with his wife
and young son, a deep long crack in reality.
Huge poetry Amazon wings: entry has arrived.

MODERNISM POSTMODERNISM NEXT

Paradigms are evident in all table of contents,
our shadowed present. Oh oh, here comes a biggie:
cleavages between modernism and postmodernism.
We argue that to treat art critics
and major buyers with Skinner boxes, simply means
that if you order the Dharma Bums
in the next eleven hours and forty six minutes,
different disciplines have adopted the terms
'it will arrive' in quite different ways.
Thinkers used to argue about the language
after human nature, would it be the end of art
if you had to give us a working definition
of the body, say, or the contribution
of foamy custard to happiness? The ongoing debate
draws some inspiration from people, but largely
to fake a few hints of interest in faces
surviving into the next generation of application.
Especially . . . that postmodernism . . .
aestheticizes everything while masquerading
as debating the validity of definitions,
I find no one in the academy
to have a catch with. One might characterize
modernism as the systematic effort
to expunge the previous slide. The broad use
of the term 'pain' suggests we have far to go
in these directions at once, such as logic
and feeling and the aesthetics of netporn.
To provide a singular notion of art,

BOB HICOK

we will hurt you with idealogies. Anyway,
back to indulging the validity of breath
as the first computer language.
Input equals going into the validity of the day
and living there in person. Who knew?

TROUBADOUR

Most people I've met would clap along
if the singer asked them to. A few
would compete with the clapper beside
    them
for the 'Most Athletic Praise in the Joint'
award, but the average vagabond is pleased
to reach one side of their life across
to the other side of their life and meet
somewhere in the middle, palms sparking
in reverence. That there are no actual
sparks doesn't stop anyone from feeling
there might be, not the flat hand
clappers or the cupped palm clappers,
who sound like horses going by in a hurry
to be happy about oats. I think I love
oats in one of their guises in a bowl
with milk. It would be good to know for
    sure,
like if a bus came by full of poets,
would you wave at the bus going by
full of poets, would you think, I know
    words
too, words like 'people exist.' They do.
It's easy to forget this, necessary
to forget sometimes the clamor-mouthed
singers and the horse clapping folk,
the shebang of the hullabaloo,
to break off a chunk of shhhh and hug
the stuffing out of it. And then, after
the sometimes, to put your mouth
against the air and fill it

with what we have to say to each other,
when it listens and then wipes
its listening clean, as if to tell us,
now try again.

BOB HICOK

THE RULES

1. THE PLAYERS

i.   According to context, the term *poem* may refer to (a) the words common to each hand or (b) the hand unique to each player.

ii. *Reader* and *Listener* are distinct players, even when occupying the same body.

iii. There must be at least two players, including the dealer (but see 3.iii).

iv. The dealer may (and initially must) occupy the same body as one of the other players.

v.   If a player leaves and returns to a game, the hand shall be deemed to be a new hand (see 2ii). No poem steps into the same reader twice.

2. THE WORDS

i.   The dealt words are common to all players.

ii. Each player also has up to five senses and a history, which may include a presence at previous deals.

iii. Certain combinations of the above may control breath, pulse, hair, and skin.

3. THE DEAL

i.   The dealer shuffles and deals the words until it is deemed that any further deal would produce an inferior hand.

ii. From this point on, the dealer has no automatic privilege over other players.

iii. A dealer who leaves the table shall nevertheless be deemed to be a player for the purposes of rule 1.iii.

iv. The game continues until the words are exhausted and/or there are no players physically present at the table.

THIRD SILENT MANIFESTO

To be someone you have to speak in one language. Having lived a number of lives at once I speak only many languages. As soon as you stop to think you think to stop. But this is not exactly how it is. One day you catch yourself just listening. Not listening for something, but listening. Then years go by and you've heard many things. You've said many things, you've thought a lot, you've visited people and places, you've wondered. You imagine that someone stops by and you try to explain. But what comes out are words that have nothing to do with what you had planned to say. You planned to say that the tropic sky is definitely blue against all that yellow. And the parakeets twitter so beguilingly that the jungle bends itself to surround them in an orange-green veil. And that the veil is then lifted and, after a shatter of lightning and rain, you fall asleep on a cot on the dark, damp porch. Your dreams contain mostly ancient images, great gods made out of stone, a woman dressed in white, an empty plate. But what actually comes out is a long sigh, a few complaints about who had said or done what about something or other, and a couple of slightly more than minor disappointments. That's all. Then you hear someone laughing—and you start to think about dinner.

FLYING: A POETICS

It is useful to distinguish between two approaches to writing. The first is to write *about* a particular subject, to record, explore, analyse or express it. The second is to write in such a way that the poem itself is the experience, or the subject. It is the second approach that I am concerned with here.

'In writing, it is not a matter of a certain material which is *there*, as a fixed thing, upon which the writing feeds and works. The act of writing also serves to nourish the material. When we speak of something, we affect it. It isn't quite the same. As we cannot altogether 'will' what we would say' (Turnbull, 1962: 27).

The process is improvisatory: to write without a set idea of where the poem is heading. As if the poem has a life, or energy, of its own.

'I just get hung on the energy. Like the way the energy goes through it' (Raworth, 1972: 12).

The poem attracts material to itself. Or, to put it another way, during writing, material finds its way in. The poem is the important thing at this stage and the language of the poem, whatever is going on in the environment, whatever thoughts occur during the writing (including memories) can dictate the direction.

Memories are stories that we tell ourselves.[1]

Though memory can appear as substantial as what is perceived as 'real' by the senses.[2]

Any experience prior to the writing of the poem is ultimately irrelevant to the poem, though the poem can 'contain' or allude to dozens of experiences.

A poem does not have to depend on the idea or experience which may have given rise to it; the idea or experience can 'merely' be the starting point.

'The poem is more than the poet's intention. The poet does not write what he knows but what he does not know. . . . Words are ambiguous. . . . The poem is not a handing out of the same packet to everyone, as it is not a thrown-down heap of words for us to choose the bonniest. The poem is the replying chord to the reader. It is the reader's involuntary reply' (Graham, 1946: 380–381).

A poem does not have to 'say' anything.

'I // have nothing to say and I am saying it / and that is poetry' (Cage, 1961: 183).

A poem may demonstrate or enact, rather than describe or explain, so that it might be difficult to say what it is 'saying'. Rather than being *about* an experience, this poem's focus is rather to provide an experience. The poem is process rather than product. [3]

'I hope the poem to *be* the subject, not *about* it' (O'Hara, 1995: 497).

Ultimately it is not possible to control the reader's response to a poem, should that be considered desirable.

'I've long since learned how little control I can have, or indeed want, over how the words in the language-field of a poem work on the association-fields of readers. All I can do is try to give the language-field a disposition, a tendency, that might point in one direction rather than another' (Fisher, 2005: 10).

A poem where language virtually demonstrates itself insufficient can take on a resonance that might be missing from a poem that is more sure of itself. [4]

By 'resonance' I mean the poem's ability to suggest interpretations: it is the suggestive capacity of the poem, a capacity which (in its range of suggestiveness) *may* call into question the poem's own ability to refer to a world outside itself.

The challenge of improvisatory writing: to write in such a way as to tap into the potential of the material, as it unfolds, to suggest further possibilities not necessarily anticipated at the beginning of the writing.

'If you know exactly what you are going to do, what is the point of doing it?' (Picasso, 1999).

Sometimes language and form appear to suggest a direction, though it *could* be that the direction suggests the language and form, *or* that the direction and the language and form together are the same impulse. The process is so subtle that it is difficult to be more precise. [5]

'FORM IS NEVER MORE THAN AN EXTENSION OF CONTENT. (Or so it got phrased by one, R. Creeley . . .' (Olson, 1950: 272). [6]

One of the most fundamental 'decisions' when starting a poem is determining the length of line. This process, in my practice, is based on the 'feel' of the poem, depending on the material and the effect.

'I don't know. I just know when I feel the line should break' (Ashbery, 1988: 199).

When I surprise myself, it's a good sign that the writing is 'going well'.

'Surprise is the greatest source of what is new' (Apollinaire, 1971: 235).

'The most modern person in Europe is you Pope Pius the Tenth,' Apollinaire wrote in 1913. Being modern was equivalent to being surprising—for about twenty years (1908–1928)' (Koch, 1998: 31). Ironically, 'My Olivetti Speaks', from which this quotation is taken, is constantly surprising, suggesting that Apollinaire is important to Koch, as he was for Frank O'Hara, and that 'surprise' is still significant, seventy years after 1928.

During the process of writing, the material can suggest a new, sometimes surprising direction. [7]

It is this method of working with which I am preoccupied: how to take the poem in an unanticipated direction, (or directions), or rather, how to get into the situation where the poem takes a new direction.

Assemblage can make the work surprising, as in the 'Emergency Rations' poems. [8]

'Emergency Rations Are Tasting Better and Better', in combining a 'realistic' text with a fictive narrative, throws the nature of the 'real' into doubt, suggesting that it is fictive, that the 'real' is only a story among other stories. The poem draws attention to the 'fictive' nature of the autobiographical voice.

Bearing in mind that it is not the job of the writer to interpret the writing: 'Being essentially the instrument for his work he (the artist) is subordinate to it and we have no reason for expecting him to interpret it for us. He has done the best that is in him by giving it form and he must leave interpretation to others and to the future' (Jung in Pound, 1967: 9). [9]

One way of allowing the poem to move in a new direction is to use improvisation in a more 'open' way by drawing on more areas of experience during the writing. [10]

'Condensing time' enables the writer to draw on the past, creating a fictive scenario in which events of different times can be treated as if they happened at the same time. [11]

Condensing time, arguably, is a kind of intuitive assemblage insofar as the poem is made out of diverse material that would not otherwise be combined were it not for the poem under construction.

The writer's experience of assemblage can affect the practice of improvisatory writing, whereby subsequent improvisations can take on the characteristics of assembled work by incorporating a wider range of apparently disparate material. [12]

The *form* of a poem can provide a significant influence. Reading Apollinaire's 'Zone' *enabled* me to write 'Thank You for the Postcard I Read It'. (Apollinaire, 1965: 20–25; Yates, 2004: 7). [13]

I was struck by the lack of enjambment in 'Zone': the technique of using the line as if it represents a new thought. Also the way in which Apollinaire uses voice in such a way as to suggest that 'he' is telling you something important and interesting, which occurs to him as he is 'talking', and that he is *enthusiastic* about it (Apollinaire, 1965: 20–25). [14]

'One thing that Frank O'Hara did was change somewhat the concept of what the subject of the poem could be. That's one of the most interesting things about his work, the whole idea of what a proper subject for a poem is . . . in Apollinaire's "Zone" the theme is whatever comes into Apollinaire's head as he is taking a walk. . . . So the subject comes close to what is in Frank's poems which is whatever is in a person's mind or whatever happens to come in front of a person in a certain span of time becomes the subject of the poem. It's very interesting in Frank's work, he takes it quite far' (Koch, 1986 in Smith, 2000: 164).

A method of writing which is attentive to language and consciously 'allowing things to happen'; rather than, for example, using language to capture and reflect on what has already happened.

'Allowing things to happen' means allowing the material to influence the direction of the poem so that one perception leads onto another, rather than imposing a direction.

Leaving out context and using juxtaposition means that there is room for the reader to supply his/her context, make connections, and provide an interpretation based upon this (or to choose *not* to do this).

Reading something exciting can give a writer *permission* to write. Some writers make you feel like writing.

O'Hara gives the impression that writing is intimate to his life and that the process of writing is not laboured: the poems read as if they are improvised, provisional, left alone when they are finished. The sense of someone *engaged in the process of writing*, who stops before making a point, thereby trusting the reader to make something with the poem.

'Every poem is a translation' or an approximation. [15]

Writing 'about' something invariably changes it.

This is most obvious, in my own practice, when attempting to write down an account of a dream soon after waking: the dream appears substantial, but as soon as words appear on the page, the sensation is that they are poor approximations of that to which they allude, that the account of the dream becomes more substantial than the memory of the dream, and appears remote from it.

This is also true, although it may appear less obvious, of writing about 'real' experience: the act of writing makes its own changes, so that the result, again, is an approximation.

'Writing makes its own demands, its own articulations, and it is its own activity—so that to say, "Why, he's simply telling us the story of his life," the very fact that he's telling of his life will be a decisive modification of what that life is. The life of the story will not so simply be the life of the man. The modifications occurring in the writing will be evident and will be significant' (Creeley, 1965: 279).

'What is experienced is lost with words, but is also reinvented with words. Words make it a new, or at least different, experience' (Kinsella, 2000: 204).

The poem is provisional. You start off saying something and language gets involved and, as soon as it does, the aeroplane's hijacked, the door's ripped off and passengers and cargo are sucked out screaming or sleeping

Or flying. [16]

'As soon as a fact is narrated no longer with a view to acting directly on reality but intransitively, that is to say, finally outside of any function other than that of the very practice of the symbol itself, this disconnection occurs, the voice loses its origin, the author enters into his own death, writing begins' (Barthes, 1968: 142).

The desire to make poems as a painter makes a painting is useful: having no fixed idea where it is going or how and when it will end. And making use of 'mistakes': 'In painting something happens—paint falls on your canvas—and you use it. Or reject it by rubbing it out' (Larry Rivers in O'Hara, 1971: 117).

To write in such a way that when you re-read the work you have no sense of the context or the thought that gave rise to it. [17] At first this is true only of more distant work that you forget you have written but with practice this can be true of poems written just a few weeks ago.

Or a few minutes ago.

'we // are // now' (Raworth, 1998: 90)

Work on a poem in such as way as to increase its interest or mystery. If leaving out context makes the poem more interesting or mysterious, leave it out. [18]

'My new theory . . . you could omit anything if you knew that you omitted, and the omitted part would strengthen the story and make people feel more than they understood' (Hemingway, 1964: 58).

Working on a poem with the energy that accompanied writing the first draft means that there is, in effect, no distinction between writing and 'drafting'. [19] 'Drafting' can open up possibilities.

'My revisions are my new works, each poem a revision of what has gone before. In-sight. Re-vision' (Duncan, 1960: 400–401).

One rule of writing (also applying to revision) which I learnt the hard way is always to stop when it is going well, when the energy is still there.

'I had learned already never to empty the well of my writing, but always to stop when there was still something there in the deep part of the well, and let it refill at night from the springs that fed it' (Hemingway, 1964: 24–25). [20]

'We cease to recognise reality. It appears to us in a totally new category, which seems to us as its own state, not ours. Apart from that state, everything in the world has been labelled. Only this is new and unlabelled. We try to give it a name. We get art.

'The clearest, most memorable and important feature of art is how it arises, and in their telling of the most varied things, the finest works in the world in fact all tell us of their own birth' (Pasternak, 1959: 213). [21]

A poem is an act of attention. The aim is to create a sense of mystery, to make the world seem new and strange.

'Our intention is to affirm this life, not to bring order out of chaos nor to suggest improvements in creation, but simply to wake us up to the very life we're living' (Cage, 1961: 95).

This is true for the artist as well as the audience; writer as well as reader. [22] Writing makes me feel alive. I write because I have to.

The next poem I write will be the most important. It will indicate the future direction of my work which I have not anticipated, either here or elsewhere. This attitude can be negative if it creates pressure and expectations which come between the writer and the writing; it is positive insofar is

CLIFF YATES

it urges the writer forward in the belief that the best is still to come.

NOTES

1 Two people can remember a shared experience differently; memories can change in the light of subsequent experience; a subsequent experience can call into question the veracity of a memory.

2 This notion is implicit in 'Baldwin Road': 'the other side of the coal bunker we built and demolished' suggests the substantiality of something that no longer exists except in memory (Yates, 2004: 28).

3 I have explored elsewhere the way in which this poetic relates to the work of Frank O'Hara and the early poems of Tom Raworth, with reference to the New American poetry and its precursors (Yates, 2006a: 123–230).

4 By 'a poem where language virtually demonstrates itself insufficient' I mean a poem where language's ability to 'capture or convey . . . experience' is called into question, as in 'Baldwin Road': 'The photographs / on the mantelpiece pull themselves together' where the cliché of 'pull yourself together' is subverted by the impossibility of giving agency to the photographs (Yates, 2004: 28). By 'a poem more sure of itself' I mean a poem that is apparently 'mimetic . . . in the general sense . . . "realistic" . . . the verbal capturing or conveying of experience in such a way that the mental image or meaning captured by the words is judged similar, analogous, or even identical to what we know about the world from sense-data directly', for example 'Meeting the Family' (Preminger and Brogan, 1993: 1038; Yates, 1999a: 50).

5 When writing on 'On the Difficulty of Learning Chinese', for example, I found myself using a particular voice, deliberate and precise, as if talking in translation, and this is reinforced by the form: starting each line, (apart from the last), with a new sentence, rather than using enjambment, as if the speaker is making one point at a time, taking care to make himself understood (Yates, 1999a: 33). The tone of this voice, formal and distant, appeared, during the writing, to generate the material.

6 Or, as Raworth says: 'Form is content stretched to whatever shape best fits' (Raworth, 1987: n.p.).

7 For example, 'Tonight in Kidderminster' starts with an improvisation based on an experience of being attacked; in the second part of the poem, a fictive sequel to the events of Stravinsky's Soldier's Tale (1918) occurs simultaneously with a surreal version of the controversial first public performance of John Cage's 4 33 , his so-called 'silent piece' (Yates, 1999a: 9–10; Cage, 1968 in Kostelanetz, 1989: 65).

8 'Emergency Rations Are Tasting Better and Better', 'On the Third Day', 'The Morning They Set Off It Was Snowing', 'Cross Country' and 'Shoes', (Yates, 2004: 11; 12; 14; 15; 16)..

9 'Writers are notoriously bad at reading their own work; indeed, that they deliberately misread it in the service of speculating about future works is a constituent of poetics' (Sheppard, 2002: 13).

10 'More areas' means not being confined by the experience or idea which provided the initial stimulus for the poem. For example 'Leswell Street', written in one sitting, combines material from widely different sources (Yates, 1999a: 25).

11 The technique of condensing time suggests that it is what is going through the mind at the writer that is significant rather than remaining faithful

to an original experience (see Koch's account of Apollinaire's writing of 'Zone' below).

12 'L'Hermitage and a Bird' illustrates the effect of experience of assemblage on improvisatory writing (Yates: 2004: 22). During the writing, there was a sense that the poem could go in any direction at any time.

13 'Thank You For The Postcard I Read It', written when I was looking for a new way of writing, started as a series of jottings and a few short, unfinished poems (Yates, 2004: 7). After reading 'Zone' the poem took on its final form.

14 Tristan Tzara also identifies Apollinaire's characteristic enthusiasm in 'Guillaume Apollinaire is Dead': 'Will the trains, the dreadnoughts, the variety theatres and the factories raise the wind of mourning for the most enduring, the most alert, the most enthusiastic of French poets?' (Tzara, 1992: 71). Stephen Dobyns attributes enthusiasm in both Apollinaire and O'Hara to the influence of Whitman (Dobyns, 1997: 69). Enthusiasm is central to my pedagogy so it is a fitting preoccupation for this text; Joe Broughton writes: 'He ... freed my imagination, really. But strangely enough, I also learned about entertaining people and stagecraft from him. We play serious music but we put it across with a spirit of fun and enthusiasm, which is exactly what he did in the classroom' (Broughton, 1999: 3).

15 'Every poem is a translation' appears in a blurb for a course which Lee Harwood and Ann Stevenson tutored, listed in the Arvon course brochure circa 1999 (details unavailable).

16 The flying metaphor is an attempt to describe the sensation that the poem has taken on a life of its own, a capacity identified by Peter Sansom as characterising 'genuine' poems: 'poems that have their own purpose, not just the writer's' (San-

som, 1999: 2). I believe that Coleridge's concept of organic form is implicit in Sansom's thinking here, as is evident in his account of 'authentic writing': 'My feeling is that the most authentic writing comes of working with more than the "conscious" thought, when the process is organic, when it relies upon—in Coleridge's phrase—the "shaping spirit of the imagination". This is still using devices, but using them instinctively and prompted by the language, the patterns a poem naturally wants to follow and develop' (Sansom, 1994: 27).

17 'The reader is the space on which all the quotations that make up a writing are inscribed without any of them being lost; a text's unity lies not in its origin but in its destination' (Barthes, 1968: 148).

18 For example, I left out references to a perceived wartime history 'behind' the poem 'L'Hermitage and a Bird': from October 1975 to January 1976, I lived in Hôtel L'Hermitage in Vittel, France, which, I was told, was used by the Gestapo during the war.

19 Working on the poem with the same sense of energy means treating the drafting stage as potentially improvisatory. See also my account of pedagogical strategies to keep the process of drafting 'fresh', which is a concern of teachers with whom I come into contact (Yates, 1999b: 14–16; 19; 45; 63; 77; 121; 130; Yates, 2007).

20 I tested out Hemingway's advice when I started to write poems in the 1980s. I have a drawer full of 'dead' poems that I overworked, keeping on writing until I was exhausted instead of stopping when it was 'going well', when the 'energy' was still there.

21 This anticipates Ashbery's comment on O'Hara: 'Frank O'Hara's concept of the poem as the

chronicle of the creative act that produces it' (O'Hara, 1995: viii–ix). For a discussion of Pasternak's statement and its importance for Ashbery's poetic as an expression of the significance of 'the situation in which [a poem] is made', or the poem's occasion, with reference also to O'Hara's notion of the occasional poem, see Herd (Herd, 2000: 7–12).

22 I am referring to my experience: this poetics is not intended to be prescriptive, neither for the author nor for the reader: 'Poetics may mismatch the writing that results. It is not necessarily a ground plan' (Sheppard, 2002: 5). A poetics is not a manifesto. In my view, the most useful function of a poetics, for other writers, is to provoke.

REFERENCES

Apollinaire, G. (1965) *Selected Poems*, Bernard, O. (ed.) (trans.) Harmondsworth: Penguin.

Ashbery, J. (1988) 'John Ashbery' interview with Peter Stitt in Plimpton, G. (ed.) *Writers at Work: The Paris Review Interviews Seventh Series*, Harmondsworth and New York: Penguin. 177–206.

Barthes, R. (1968) 'The Death of the Author' in *Image-Music-Text: Essays Selected and Translated by Stephen Heath*, (1977) Glasgow: Collins, Fontana.

Broughton, J. (1999) 'My Best Teacher' in *Times Educational Supplement: TES Friday*, 18 June. 3.

Cage, J. (1961) *Silence*, 2nd British edition (1987) London: Marion Boyars.

Dobyns, S. (1997) *Best Words, Best Order: Essays on Poetry*, 2nd edition, New York: St. Martin's Griffin.

Duncan, R. (1960) 'Pages from a Notebook' in Allen, D. (ed.) *The New American Poetry 1945–1960*, 2nd edition (1999) Berkeley: University of California Press. 400–407.

Fisher, R. (2005) 'Behind the Poem' [interview] in *The Poetry Paper*, Issue 2.

Graham, W. S. (1946) 'Notes on a Poetry of Release' in Snow, M. and M. (eds.) (1999) *The Nightfisherman: Selected Letters of W. S. Graham*, Manchester: Carcanet

Herd, D. (2000) *John Ashbery and American Poetry*, Manchester: Manchester University Press.

Hemingway, E. (1964) *A Moveable Feast*, Harmondsworth: Penguin. 1973.

Jung, C.G. (1967) quoted in 'Introduction', Pound, E. *The Selected Cantos of Ezra Pound*, London: Faber and Faber. 9.

Kinsella, J. (2000) 'Almost a Dialogue with Lyn Hejinian: Quotations with Phantom Limbs . . .' in Herbert, W.N., and Hollis, M. (2000) *Strong Words: Modern*

Poets on Modern Poetry, Tarset: Blood-axe. 203–207.

Koch, K. (1998) Straits: *Poems by Kenneth Koch*, New York: Alfred A. Knopf.

Kostelanetz, R.(ed.) (1989) *Conversing with Cage*, 2nd edition, London, New York, Sidney: Omnibus Press.

O'Hara, F. (1971) *Art Chronicles 1956–1966*, 2nd edition, New York: George Braziller.

Olson, C. (1950) 'Projective Verse' in Scully, J. (ed.) (1966) *Modern Poets on Modern Poetry*, London: Fontana/Collins. 270–282.

Perloff, M. (1966) *Wittgenstein's Ladder: Poetic Language and the Strangeness of the Ordinary*, Chicago: University of Chicago Press.

Picasso, P. (1999) 'If you know exactly what you are going to do, what is the point of doing it?' Text on a postcard accompanying a photograph by Robert Doisneau. Paris: Rapho Éditions Hazan. Succession Picasso CN 5150.

Preminger A. and Brogan, T.V.F. (eds.) (1993) *The New Princeton Encyclopedia of Poetry and Poetics*, 3rd edition, Princeton, New Jersey: Princeton University Press.

Raworth, T. (1972) 'Tom Raworth—An Interview' by Barry Alpert' reprinted in (1998) *Tom Raworth: An Exhibition of Book- and Art-Works*, Cambridge: Cambridge Conference of Contemporary Poetry. Separately paginated 1–16.

Raworth, T. (1987) 'Letters from Yaddo' in *Visible Shivers*, Oakland, Calif.: O Books, in association with Trike.

Raworth, T. (1988) *Tottering State: Selected Poems 1963–1987*, 2nd edition, London, Paladin.

Raworth, T. (2003) *Collected Poems*, Manchester: Carcanet.

Sansom, P. (1994) *Writing Poems*, Newcastle: Bloodaxe Books.

Sansom, P. (1999) 'Editorial' in *The North*, 25.

Sheppard, R. (2002) *The Necessity of Poetics*, Liverpool: Ship of Fools.

Smith, H. (2000) *Hyperscapes in the Poetry of Frank O'Hara: Difference / Homosexuality / Topography*, Liverpool: University of Liverpool.

Turnbull, G. (1962) 'Resonances & Speculations upon reading Roy Fisher's City' In *Kulchur*, New York, II, 7. Autumn. 23–29.

Tzara, T. (1992) 'Guillaume Apollinaire is Dead' in *Seven Dada Manifestos and Lampisteries*, Wright, B. (trans.) Lon-

CLIFF YATES

don, Paris, New York: Calder Publications; Riverrun Press.

Yates, C. (1999a) *Henry's Clock*, Huddersfield: Smith/Doorstop.

Yates, C. (1999b) *Jumpstart Poetry in the Secondary School*, 2nd edition 2004. London: Poetry Society.

Yates, C. (2004) *Emergency Rations*, Huddersfield: Smith/Doorstop.

Yates, C. (2006a) 'The Poem as Process: Theory and Practice.' Unpublished PhD thesis: Edge Hill University (University of Lancaster).

Yates, C. (2006b) 'Vienna' in The North, 36.

Yates, C. (2007) 'Writing Like Writers in the Classroom: Free Writing and Formal Constraint' in *English in Education* Vol. 41 No. 3.

THE RAW EDGE BLUES

what we want, he said,
is writing with a raw edge
that tears off a strip
that blisters the lips

that rips
that chips
    off the old block
exposing a vision espied
at the stone heart

whittles barriers to
souvenirs and reunification

writing that gives those clean paper cuts
that annoy with their tingling precision
exposing your mendicant flesh
to inspection
whose incision is clinical and remorseless

that brings the joyful discomfort of puberty
the sleepless nights of discovery

that
    dances from the wrist
like a twister

whose ink is
the cliff's plunging down
to the sea
the quarry's crumbling brow

the brink
the verge

the barbed wire between entrenched
positions
       cradling the wounded on
its points

the margin
the coping

where the avalanche begins
where ice-bergs break free
where night hushes into streaks

      ~

I woke up this morning just about the dawn
I was tossing and a turnin' like a feather in a
storm
There was a raw edge to my pillow, thought
I'd never sleep no more
There was a raw edge to my pillow,
      I thought I'd never sleep no more

GHOST MACHINE
SELF-ASSEMBLY KIT

DAVE BIRCUMSHAW

INSTRUCTIONS

I FUEL RECIPE

Take three quarts of paradox from your nearest pint-pot. Add essence of dementia. Stir briskly and pepper with molecules. Allow to stand and wait for imagination to rise. Knead two gross of nebulae into a malleable pastry. Add one poppet of whatever-it-is, a broad sauce of parody and a prime choice cut of indignant indigence. Stand well back and light fuse. Never look directly at the sun.

II CHASSIS ASSEMBLY

Retrieve bones from elephants' graveyards. Collect rusting girders from derelict factories. Connect elephant bones (A) to girders (B) using risible appliance (enclosed). Next mount with the best available 'saurian fossil (*Triceratops* recommended) and decorate with leaves torn from *The World's Classics*. Test for balance and dynamics with an improbalometer (not enclosed). Remember, you must not take it out onto the streets or to social functions until you have obtained a proper licence.

III POWERING UP

Once cooled, remove fuel from centre of crater. Apologize to your neighbours for demolition of their homes. (*Hope they renewed their insurance!*) Next, taking just a sufficient amount, in exactly the *right place*, never elsewhere, pour in a quantity of fuel. When the red indicator flashes on, scram. Beware of ephemera *and* stolid, wooden objects for the first five minutes. If elephants persist, consult your local dealer.

IV DRIVING YOUR MACHINE

Avoid right turns. Be considerate to other users, particularly the elderly and bicyclists. Take care at junctions, there may be an unexpected development. At all times be humane, remember, machines have feelings too. Watch out for time-hoppers and avoid being caught in their slipstream. Regularly check your appearance in a mirror—in case of sudden change immediately turn off your Ghost Machine. Do not run engine while standing still as a personal morass might appear, particularly in the vicinity of a carpet.

HIS STORY —
ONE VERSION

Tired, said the author, and looked down at his *open quite empty hands.* A yellow-beaked bird eyed him without interest on the table. It's not like it used to be—it was better writing poems, complained our former poet.

Yellow-beak pointed forward. It begins with poems, it said, all the stories start with *waves* and *particles* of rhythm. In the first days there were poems. You make poems sound like nursery rhymes, the defender of verse declared. 'Ding dong bell'—returned yellow-beak —Sprung rhythm equals high poetic culture. Sophomore, snapped poet.

Yellow-beak's black-button eyes watched without emotion as the twin halves of poet struggled to re-unite on the floor. OK, gasped the author, breathless, returning to his feet, You win—poetry can't take the tension, it can't carry its own strain. But what about this? —he continued—waving his arms at the grimy room—It's drab, it's dull, I can't stand it.

Beginning with nursery rhymes and fairy stories, the bird recited, *human* life progresses to awareness of self and others through the development of sympathetic imagination. For this we need, not the high-tension flashes of lyric verse, its *detonations*, not the audio-visual storms of celluloid, not the mindless intelligence of music, but the quiet persistence of prose.

Thanks for the sermon, said man to bird. It's too much like work, he moaned. The laws of thermodynamics, hummed the bird. Exactly, I hate them, protested the anti-physicist. Become a fifth-columnist, you'll like it, suggested black-button eyes.

Oh I *like* that—become a *traitor*—what a career move, sneered the loyal scribe.

OK then—call yourself The Resistance, chirped the bird.

I'll think about it, our hero conceded.

You'll go on? asked the feathered comforter.

All right, I said, but later, I *am* tired.

The bird disappeared from print without a word and I sat in my room alone.

But why tell stories, I asked the bird in my mind.

Because of the terrible fact, it replied.

DAVE BIRCUMSHAW

INSTRUCTIONS FOR
A GOOD TIME

DAVID HART

1. Wait by the great horse chestnut, wait simply.

2. Give up waiting and mooch around by the pool in tears.

3. Put on a handy uniform and march about the front room alone singing boldly.

4. Bounce along the path memorising Tennyson for fun.

5. Shuffle your papers and look out to watch the high incoming tide.

6. Rush to post a letter bearing no name or address only a kiss and a smiley face.

7. Abandon the picnic to search for where the bee sucks.

8. Clear the tennis court of flying fish.

9. Sing to yourself on the stairs step by step up then down.

10. Find an historic courtyard and wander about in it all night thinking up instructions for a good time.

A clerk will bring chairs.

FOURTH SILENT MANIFESTO

I the person had so much to say, while I the author wished only silence. I the person had problems like anybody else—sick of paying bills, tired of pains in the feet, no time to read and more importantly no time to think, eating too much and worrying too much, grateful to but irritable with friends, never enough sunny days, hard to make a decision, have I lived up to my potentials, am I a good mate, is my mate a good mate, am I a good parent, were my parents any good, did I mean what I said, do I say what I mean;—while I the author has different problems like what are my themes, is death for real, what is the nature of time, are my characters in conflict, do my sentences get to the point, am I boring, am I popular, is my book a good read, where do I start a work and how do I end it, is all this worth all the trouble, is my agent telling the truth or lying, are my friend's books better than mine, are my old poems better than my new ones . . . so I the author wishes to be silent. And I the person wants to talk . . .

NICK PIOMBINO

ROXY: SECTION 34

GAVIN SELERIE

Heretical figures put our concepts on trial.
Have we eaten the heart, to have no other
    taste?
I had a dream till a movement killed it,
I had a movement till a dream killed it.
I was an actor warming frozen words.
I was a word warming a frozen actor.

A revolution of 180 degrees
is the sentence coming into being.
Who, then, is the cell animator?

Production is the watchword now
structured for the average reader,
whatever that means. With workers
    redundant,
golden apples are comfortably outlandish
if they're printed right into the gutter.

To speak with sense
you hold your nose or your purse.

The soul's palace is erected wit
without any sparkle of light.
Her diverting parts are a piece
of mere manage, an idea twirled
into a costly thatch.

Take off this value-language
for under that you may see beauty.

Gold and silver. You speak as if
they were an illusion and the orchard not.

I'd rather set myself in your green-house
than in the cold gallery of fashion.

It was settled once with bottles and chairs,
by a landrover driven up a poet's boot.

That was before helicopter blades
lifted the pages of corporate ink.

Flying with the last drop, there's no
    further
to go on. It's a heart map, a fool's head
    world.

Oil beneath tracing sings a hymn
    momently
coloured to cry what's new.

Feathers are a burden, unfinished as fable
and tranced into a glaze.

You can hide with floating letters.

The voiced valise is no picture
but sometimes a tool to point the pretence
it's convenient enough to follow.

We walk dumpily away from the drivel
while others cover, endow, commit.

In the end they're all the same—
just different uniforms.

Style is what you can't deny
about yourself.

MANIFESTO TO MYSELF

GEOFF STEVENS

A poem is an excuse to oneself
for not travelling widely
for inactivety in love
for not saving favourite places from destruction
for not fighting for one's beliefs because of the
odds.
It is an excuse for not being a train driver
for not being Prime Minister
for not playing cricket for England
for not being a famous artist
musician
novelist
actor
It is an excuse to oneself
and it often depends on how convincing it
needs to be
on how good a poem it is

MANIFESTO OF THE
SELF-PUBLICISTS

Sir/Madam,

We are a coalition of younger market makers and interested parties who wish to see our industry develop its potential for realist-centred change within the context of the society in which we find ourselves. We therefore set out below our vision of its creatably successful future.

We envisage our target audience as 25–60, left-leaning, appreciative of irony, probably employed in the education sector and/or connected with the 'literary' world in some professional manner (perhaps part-time); home-owning (or aspirationally so); intelligent, educated to degree level, and familiar with the leading brandnames currently in the market.[1]

We hope to offer a range of product which should reflect the desires and aspirations of this group in terms of

(a)   subject[2]

(b)   form

(c)   attitude[3]

with the following key provisions, namely:

• rigorous time-management workflow by means of adherence to preagreed formulae[4] (which may subsequently be tailored to individual needs if required and/or pertinent)

• recognisable product identity within a prespecified range of choice

• advertised reiteration of product benefits ('self-improvement', 'appreciation of "beauty"', 'cultural prop to bourgeois lifestyle' &c)

thus ensuring

1)   maximisation of product marketability (notwithstanding neo-ideological concepts of critical 'quality'—except insofar as this increases the former)

2)   efficiency, viability, professionalism, media-relations (ditto)

3)   'love' of 'language'

GUY RUSSELL

GUY RUSSELL

We believe that such a poetics is the only one truly of its time.

Thank you for your attention.[5]

THE SELF-PUBLICISTS

PS
We deplore, it goes without saying, the current state of poetry in this country.

NOTES

1 Armitage; Duffy; Harrison; &c

2 Antecedent research detects resistance of target group to (*inter alia*): death of pets; adolescent bedrooms; amusing sayings of grandchildren; shards; sunsets.

3 See target audience. 'Attitude' may be deemed appropriate, esp. among lower-income sectors.

4 With regard to the factors outlined above, we believe that increased productivity, in today's highly competitive market, is the only way to preserve the UK's economic position and safeguard jobs in this sector.

5 To join *The Self-Publicists*, send only £49.99 (inc. p+p) to the Secretary at 3 Helicon Gardens, London, WC1 4RT for free membership card and personally-printed copy of manifesto.

MANIFESTO (1995)

1. Spiritualism. Never assume that in attacking something as religious, you are not part of a religion yourself. Jung not Freud.

2. If you are going to use the I-Ching, notice how your interaction with it produces a different work than is produced by someone else using the I-Ching. Notice that your works are more like each other, than your I-Ching works are like I-Ching works by other artists. Stockhausen not Cage.

3. Keep listening.

5. Have Pound's decency to look back on what you've represented. Next Generation not Kirk.

8. If improvisation is free, why do many of its evenings go out to the same boundary and no further? Leibniz not Newton.

13. To lecture, Stein milking not mocking a restrained common vocabulary to write descriptions, not Derrida punning and concatenating with abstracts to provoke, always with fixed unspoken loyalties of his own, and not own explicitly. Close to who you pretend?

21. Non-Freudian not neo-Freudian post-structuralism, if any.

34. Gloria Steinem not Julia Kristeva.

55. Fuck gender-fuck, open up genre. Harryman not Silliman. Thresh hold of 'becoming' an adult and 'no longer' being like a child. Neil Gaiman not Ridley Scott. Nurture, non-sexual love sexual life; actual practice of community, professor. Elizabeth Burns' *Letters to Elizabeth Bishop*, not Derrida's *The Post Card*.

89. Hyper-reality and reality, extend, object both ways. Posters and paintings of words not handwritten notebooks. Brush syntax. Johanna Drucker meets Emily Dickinson.

144. The sentence was a good stretch, but now I choose my jailors. Sing energy. So long when you misuse lyric poetry as a prison term. 'The voice makes possible the entire continuum from the most extreme consonant-like noises to the purest vocal sound, and is far superior to even the most modern apparatus for creating tone-colours'. Stockhausen not Zukofsky, the musical phrase, remember, not the metronome.

BOTHER

'What do you want? Is the poem a pony?'
Rachel Blau DuPlessis, 'Draft 9: Page'

JANIS BUTLER HOLM

I

The word is my leopard.

Spaces between
are yielding
to vertigo.

I shell nuts, gaunt.

Darks of misgrace.

We take meth, pee,
shoo flies, drown
in mean raptures.

Those seismic nude grievances
have their indifferences.

We pee meth, flee,
deride the shrill otters.

Close your cellar-door
splendor. Sing the result.

We adore meth, lie cold.

II

When you cling, I want spires or infinite potato cake. The kind I can barter. Why the hell not? Thirty ways to pick the fuzz from old books and radios. What's left for looking isn't a clue.

If slack skin's your metaphor, choose the banana bread. As if words were fingers. Ha. Odalisque this. It's not what I respected, but tell me whenever. Just another detail for the socially blank.

You're saying what's she got that I can happily exonerate. Maybe yellow birds or other rough trade. Azure, as you like it. Like I care about caring. Maybe our sponsor had the ugly ones dumped.

You're stupid or snappy or possibly history. How not to murmur while the rest of it grows. That's what they get for charming my envelope. Consider the hassle: spitting out flak.

III

Er erquicket meine Seele.

We cooed
and delivered.

Li fè m' reprann fòs.

My little
scud epistle.

Confortará mi alma.

She yearns for the clamor
of mountainous roadies,
all squeaky-mean
in extravagant pants.

IV

On those three ____ hang all my ____ and all my ____ when it comes to ____ the ____ for ____. I trust to be able to remember the ____ for a ____ or an exclamation ____, or a question ____ to mark the ____ of my ____, or a ____ when, in rare ____, I want to introduce a formal ____ or ____.

Can we not induce them to remember the exterior ____, and to think so clearly that only an occasional ____ will become necessary, and to see that, when the ____ *does* demand a ____, it is to be used, not as a ____ possessing ____ in itself, any more than ____, but because without it some ____ may not possess sufficient suggestive ____, and to feel that a straight ____often conveys an ____ better than a ____ of explanatory ____? Or must we go on giving the ____ ____ in ____ by ____ and continue to wonder why they do not see that they are not punctuating with ____?*

JANIS BUTLER HOLM

JANIS BUTLER HOLM

V

After sunrise,
a sky of guitars.

Plunder the goat,
or plunder the pack.

When are calliopes
rounder than silver?

Whose blunt ornament,
guttery psalm?

VI

       redolent   quiver

            lapis
gordo

               crypt
                  Dasein

    fragment
Urdu

          shift
     languor   *merde*

   apostate   stick

        et

VII

A meandering of ciphers, curly and straight,
a consequence of memory where hair categories and quiet dislike make an excelsior,
cushioning reliance on telltale encounters that
could be enough, however hard you struggle
to mount the thick air.

VIII

Yesterday rained more gladly.
His fear held clever color.
They were dear in a bad way.
You wore your skin aloft.

NOTES

* This text derives from E. Dudley Parsons's 'Bow-
ing Down before the God of Punctuation,' *English
Journal* 4 (1915): 598–99.

IF YOU MUST HAVE NOUNS

Is it you, Dionysios Thrax? Or shall I denounce Panini?
Syntax and *techne*, grammar and name, I'll show you mine if you take the blame
The head of a noun-phrase thinking, the tail all baptised in light
Yet samely they frightened abundance—
Capital and count, proper and mass, collective, concrete and abstract
The algebra aided and alphabeted, now a parcel of gestalt rogues,
A sequitur of dribbling logicians—
Moment by moment, breath by breath, the wordfall is drifting
On angular winds, blowing up gullies of wicked scorched metal,
Sciencing under the microworld, for a slice of telluric miasm

In abeyance hangs the gilded shaft of unformed morning, aching
For wordless worlds and time, unminded, leaf-tiled
In a tremendous swash of autumn red and brown against the greening
Turn of dawn, the spreading wave of weed and breeze
Seeding succession, plutonic shoots giving rat-muscle sinuous pushing,
Wild effort under pavement and tarmac, effortless glimpses of the crack
Leonard mentioned, and we chose fruitfully to ignore

Split mystery, and our spilt history of life-ways traded and invalidated
Always from a throne, a dominator's home, where higher arches
And hired archers, with rafters descended to ruin, like the abandoned hall
Broken open, rusting arrows on Sundays in November,
The silent fall of this lamentable present

Or songlines, eked from Earthdeep, tended and burrowed
Watered with foreskins, peeled against starlight once brighter than day
Where ancestors whisper at cornucopias, leathermen chew bridles of despair
Creationists stalk the Vodafone wavelengths, censoring diamonds with coaldust
As the tribe unfolds, understanding everything now
Refuses its neo-con cure-all, smiles at the phantom presidents on the tip of the mushroom

KEITH HACKWOD

The tribe condenses in still-to-be, vapour tendrils by the mercury sea,
Boiling up shells for a prime lime surrender
A world of tender shells, dusty crustacean once-upon-a-time-ness
Porous with serpentine knowing, organ-pipe cacti lapping cool juices, oh, such love!

Medicine! Medicine! The people cry beside themselves, forgetting that the SS
Burned the medicine, that allopathic whitecoats always lay claim to virtue
Medicine! Medicine! The tribe is refuge made refugee by white magic that is actually black,
By the nouns you insisted we speak (though we knew their tendency for telling lies, taking
pleasure in the act of lying) 'In the beginning was the noun' —
And the noun was our idiot self, our soft-lobed cunt-hearted poet-fool art-self,
Now bastardised as munchkins and cancerous pumpkins flowing down the undead ages, Squir-
reling up an aeon of hot knotted wire and devilish wet electrics, or
Passing geodes filled with the blood of witches, scribbling sensible edicts to the music of Whip-
hand screeches; electrode intrusions, rubber truncheons
The sharp edge of tomorrow's promise draws across the slender cherry's throat —

The Pinocchio dog is sniffing our crotches — be careful what you wish for,
This is just run-off and outgassing, wet work for revenue-protection operatives
John Lackland is whoring Miss Magna Carta, auctioning souls to the daughters of torture
Mr Peacekeeper, sir, will you take me to the euphemism now?

MANIFESTO

1

my name has been reassembled by officials
my name will hold up walls
my name falls lost between constellations
my name cannot be unlocked
my name is the real name for someone
      who is called by another name
my name can look at a king
my name opens
my name fell down many stairs
my name is vapour
my name poisons the dreams of my
      enemies
my name grows in spring
my name has lost itself in surf
my name is searching for a splendid kite
my name is not for anyone
my name connects me to my name
my name has let loose her dogs
my name ran off on a boy
my name has died and been born
my name has ceased to be a word
my name falls from the sky
my name is addicted to mouths
my name feasts on blue
my name rests
my name flies from me when i look at the
      baby and i am no one always
my name climbs slowly back up the
      mountain
my name has accepted me

2

our collective is best in water
our collective may help you forget
our collective has learnt to evade the
      cyclops
our collective laughed its head off
our collective heard music
our collective let bob scream
our collective has a new hoover
our collective rode upon a seashell
our collective is not a theory but can be
our collective will let the world take over
our collective falls in autumn
our collective called to the mermaids
our collective gently waits
our collective has a tunnel that reaches
      california
our collective is the sound of a boatyard
our collective changes everything
our collective is inflammable
our collective saw the ceaseless connecting
      rain
our collective works night
our collective cannot be located
our collective uses chalk
our collective makes soft mistakes
      properly into pleasuredomes
our collective was never a prefect
our collective is swift

KEITH JAFRATE

our collective digressed into the grass and
    vanished
our collective survived

3

we release
we carefully uncover the lullaby of
    persephone drinking at her mother's
    breast
we fill the glass of the self with ozone
we lead words up the garden
we abandon the minotaur in a foreign
    maze
we bring strong coffee
we sing
we are discovered forgetting the plot
we wake among nettles
we remember the white dawn of passage
we enter the mist of pebbles
we set fire to the diary of milk
we work with pieces missing
we encounter our ignorance at the edge of
    the concert
we leap into impeccable shadows
we place the weary heart in a sunlit
    window
we laugh
we give our secrets to a mouse
we make costumes stronger than hate
we build kites in impractical alleyways

we watch the burden of the moon rise
we open the door of the veins of leaves
we witness the compromise of all winged
    things
we fly
we return
we have more to tell

4

we want lovers
we want giants
we want more cakes
we want berserk survivors
we want the pencil of earthquakes
we want pure ignorance
we want the screams of the lost boy rolling
    in dust
we want chords of light stepping over
    moorland
we want bare feet
we want that listening which is dissolution
we want girl flame
we want the lunar propulsion of improv
we want the sinuous machine of grass
we want magi
we want that flower which is the moment
    of departure
we want to submit to the butterfly
we want the birds of voice to nest in us
we want to descend into a silence of

poplars
we want the broken ornaments of surf
we want a city a whole city
we want a window of rain
we want the small hesitations of the moth
    to matter
we want that unbreakable blue hawser the
    sky tows eyes with
we want singers
we want witches
we want earth

5

we do not want the iron wig of success
we do not want the eye on legs and its
    search for ever bigger mirrors
we do not want the flogging or the dead
    horse
we do not want the jet engine and its
    capuccino
we do not want the story of the radical
    armchair
we do not want the fresh-faced beelzebub
we do not want the bloodstained postcard
we do not want the debonair bailiff
we do not want the inspector of
    vocabularies
we do not want the bicep of truth
we do not want the muffled surgeon

we do not want the jealous stone
we do not want the endless murmuring of
    those in flight from the facts
we do not want the facts jack just the facts
we do not want the jack of sharks
we do not want the democratically elected
    collection of dead butterflies
we do not want the doubleglazed tribune
    of the people's whim
we do not want the community rhino
we do not want the endless crumbs
we do not want the lecture on betrayal
we do not want the happiness of statues
we do not want the census of our blood
    returned to us
we do not want the balanced analysis
we do not want the retired snake
we do not want the leadership of tombs
we do not want the pitiless certainty of the
    blessed

AUTOMATIC MANIFESTO #5

NICK PIOMBINO

A poem must be aged like wine. Nothing more bitter or hard to taste than a new poem. Yet poets live in the delirium of new poems. The intoxication of the new consists, in part, of its role of proffering evidence of the aliveness of the form and the experiential actualities of the present.

Death is a constant presence for the reader of poems. Such names as Donne, Marvell, Blake, Stevens, Zukofsky, Stein moving towards and away from us at the speed of light. 'Nature is an infinite sphere whose centre is everywhere and circumference nowhere.' (Pascal)

Human work consists of learning to remember. But first we must learn to allow that all of us—and everything—exists at the same time.

In this poem the poet is telling us that learning to love language is learning to not be deflated by the omnipresence of clichés. The cult of the new makes an idol out of strangeness. What is eternally new is perception leading to insight. It is insight that turns what might have been a cliché into something substantial. A cliché is a failed attempt at insight.

The poem asks: where is the poem? Where is the poetry located? The poet first identifies a significant event amounting to an obsession. Is a truth to be found here? Yes, because this is what the surroundings themselves consist of.

Unless you ask me I don't know why I do it, I just do it. I keep feeling for it until I get it right. It's like reaching for a plug in the dark. If you need a lamp to plug in the lamp you might get stuck at the start.

I wasn't exactly 'listening' either. I was just there. I didn't want to say about it, I just wanted to say it. Psychoanalysis and literature are more interrelated than is apparent. This is pretty close to the source of the current emanations. A sort of writing as preparedness or meta-communication. It is a meeting of the meanings.

Psychoanalysts don't need more case literature. The writing should embrace all the meanings and experiences, not only scientific explanations. This takes us into new territory. We may feel impelled to go towards a kind of writing that embraces *whole* selves not just trackings of the unconscious self, an idiom more akin to new poetry than old science.

DECONSTRUCTIONISM IS NOT ENOUGH; OR A QUEST TO DISCOVER WHY I STUTTER WHEN A STRANGER ASKS ME MY NAME

This is a love letter to Michel Foucault:

Dearest Fou-Fou,

If I were gay and you were gay and you let me say the word gay and if you could last for thirty seconds without laughing in my face for using the word love then I would say **I love you**. If I survived your endless scrutiny of what I mean by 'I' and 'you' and whether I enjoy submitting to systems of arbitrary entrapment then I would look into your grey eyes and once more say **I love you**. If I could prove to you that I did not wish to capture you or to project my faults through dominance through the device of love then I would shout I love you. If I could dissect your name from your actions and escape talking of you as an author or you as a body or you as a neurotic gaunt bold man and I came to terms with the fact that I was merely employing metaphors for unreachable concepts through a hierarchical frame then I would kiss your shiny scalp and scream I LOVE YOU.

It is with unkind irony that art should find absolute freedom as science finds its absolute impossibility. I say this with a tone of prophecy rather than actuality. It is impossible to imagine what form absolute freedom might take. One might be drawn to defining absolute freedom (in literature at least) as the ability to do and say whatever you like however you like. This seems to be the ultimate aim of postmodernism. But why? These writers reflect on freedom itself but freedom is a negative, a lack. Squaring negatives creates very big unreal positives: guilt, depression; not happiness. Our current age lacks a narrative within which individuals can find their place. People aren't interested in books anymore. What is it to subscribe to freedom or equality? How could these negatives be relevant to our lives? The deconstructionist plays the role of a seven year old with a screwdriver who bitterly disassembles his toy robot only to say 'See! It only moves because of the engine', as if that changes the robot somehow. Of course the whole is a sum of its parts. Of course a woman is a woman because she acts as a woman just as a waitress is only a waitress as far as she walks rigidly and offers you a wine list. Of course there is no underlying essence, no ultimate truth, no magic that makes the robot talk! This should be a simple and necessary assumption rather than the final aim. Deconstructionists are still devout Christians with a God-shaped hole in their thinking. All this is natural. This is entropy. Everything in the universe must decay. Particles become increasingly more random with time, thus the extreme becomes the average, thus the potential difference between areas of particles

KYRILL POTAPOV

decreases, thus energy between particles decreases, thus matter dies. That is if matter is all that exists in this universe, that freedom is all that is worth fighting for.

I will not speak of ultimates but only of sufficients. There is one clear concept which sufficiently does not fit within the post-modern schema to destroy it. Laughter. Nothing is funny within itself. You can not deconstruct what is funny, only the mechanics and semantics of the idea of a joke. What pointless and arbitrary behaviour laughter seems to be and yet it is our direct instinctive response to the way that things relate to each other: a forever fleeting yet always present relationship. A joke is a clear plot on the graph of random infinity; proof that a line can be drawn.

Freedom is imperative but only as something implicit within the whole. We must always keep our freedom and responsibility but still leave enough to be responsible *for*. Let us be thankful that we have no absolutes or perfections. Stupidity is the one advantage we have over animals. Let us not just dig up soil but let us build houses within the foundations. Let us be Constructionists.

My ancestors are fishermen. My dad is called Alexander Alexandrevitch Potapov and his dad is called Alexander Alexandrevitch Potapov and his dad is called Alexander Alexandrevitch Potapov. Potapov is a name given to bears as Rover is for dogs in this country. The bear is a symbol of Russia and a symbol of subtle might and craftsmanship. Alexander is also a Russian symbol. It symbolises kingship and loyalty and once more subtle might. My ancestors caught this perfectly with every sturgeon in their nets. But here I am. Kyrill Potapov. In England. I spent today listening to Slam poetry and eating cod and chips from Don's Fish and Chips. My dad did not act equal. He moved from the Steppes of near Outer Mongolia to Moscow. This was at a time when Communist Russia was questioning the cost of freedom. He wanted to become a photographer. He succeeded. The last I heard from him was on my 18th birthday in one e-mail which said (as I translate it) 'Happy Birthday. Hope you are well, I am back in Astrakhan. Your dad.' Attached to the e-mail was an e-book called 'The Aims of Patriots', outlining how one must stick to one's call in society to be happy. It was trashy. I deleted it.

Pulp fiction aside, my dad left me one very important thing: my name. I was named after my grandmother, Keira; 'Kyrill' is the closest male equivalent. Kyrill means 'first founder'. The man who brought the Russian language to Russia was called Kyrill. That means he was the first Russian writer. You've got to laugh (drawing lines, remember?).

My current creative writing piece was inspired by a homeless man with a blanket over his knees. He had an old Sprite bottle in one hand and in the other a copy of Nietzsche's *Twilight of the Idols*. It really happened. It was under Westgate. With this in mind, I set to writing an authentic reply to the image. I got home and drew my curtains and closed my door and sat on my bed meditating. I tried not to let any meaning enter my head. The image I had seen earlier would undoubtedly effect the actions of my subconscious mind but I still tried to make my conscious mind as clear as possible. All I wanted was a phrase or a collection of words as a starting point for my piece. If they alone were authentic, I would be happy. I spent about twenty minutes in meditation with various words entering my head until one phrase finally resonated within me. I let the group of words come into my mind's eye and then grabbed a pad and pen to write them down. The words were this:

'cats are bad'

I then started to free associate. In what sense were cats bad? I thought of Top Cat, the cat criminal from the cartoon. But this was just one special example of a cat and besides, he wasn't bad, he was endearing. What I wrote was 'cats' and not 'cat'. It seemed to be calling to an ultimate archetype of a cat rather than any specific group of cats or situation involving cats. In what way then can cats be said to be bad? A cat may break a vase or bring home a dead vermin. Here however, it is only the reaction of a human which could be seen as bad and not the actual essence of the cat. How can a cat be bad from the point of view of cat? Well surely it can not. Only humans can be bad. The only way a cat can be bad is if it ceases to be a cat: in other words, if it gets itself killed. There is a further science-fiction possibility; for example the cat may somehow turn itself into another creature but I will dismiss this alternative for now. So it is now clear that in my plot a cat needs to get itself killed and as I can not subjectively access a cat, not being a cat myself, it also means that in the plot a human needs to be turned bad by the death of the cat. Since it is the ideology of cats which I am setting out as bad in my aim, my first sentence needs to kill the archetype of a cat; perhaps as follows:

'One thing you should know straight off is that there never was a cat.'

From here, the narrative will naturally flow. Obviously, what I really want is to destroy, or perhaps live up to, the ideology of my name and to find at the end of it that my life is not bad like cats but somehow positive and right; to not worry that when I tell someone my name they will say 'that's interesting, where is it from?' Maybe the reason why I stutter uncontrollably when a stranger asks for my name is, I need to squeeze *all this* through the space of two soft syllables.

Yours Truly,
Kyrill.

TOWARDS A MANIFESTO
FOR A NEW POETRY

Poetry should:

1. Refuse to be reduced to an 'ism'

2. Fly in the face of convention, except where it feels impelled to embrace it

3. Reject all snobbery and effete-ism, except to ridicule it

4. Be blatantly random

5. Be not afraid to be unreadable

6. Be not afraid to be abstract

7. Be not afraid to be vulgar, angry, political or annoying

8. Reject all notions of craft

9. Be not afraid to be funny

10. Be unafraid to be humble

11. Be unafraid

12. Be useless

13. Be unpublishable

14. Be written without regard to set notions of art, artifact, or above all, the artist's place in history

15. Be handwritten

16. Include hypertext, if desired

17. Be as easily performed as ballet as spoken word

18. Be in blatant violation of FCC regulations

19. Contain genuine emotion

20. Be written for people, dogs, rocks, fruit . . .

21. Be exclusively auditory

22. Be exclusively visual

23. Be exclusively excrement

24. Be pleasurable

25. Be difficult

26. Be easy

27. Be academically unsound

28. Be chemically unstable

29. Be cruel

30. Be humane

LAEL EWY

31. Be blasphemous

32. Be holy

33. Be heavy

34. Be cream

35. Be blue

36. Be pink

37. Be red.

A MANIFESTO TOWARDS
REPEATING THE MISTAKES
OF THE PAST

1. Nobody is FORCING you to use epigraphs.

    1.1 'Nobody is *forcing* you to use epigraphs.' — Luke Kennard, 'A Manifesto Towards Repeating the Mistakes of the Past'

2. For every event you read at, try to go to two events where you're not on the billing. If you find the ratio weighed towards the former, ask yourself: Am I actually interested in poetry? Or do I just like people clapping after my name?

    2.1 Keep an Excel spreadsheet that gauges your sense of self-importance over a three year time period. You will know where to set the parameters. Should it exceed them turn to stand-up comedy for immediate defusing.

3. Poetry about sex, drugs and violence was actually pretty big in Ancient Greece. Never say that you are going to 'shake up the literary establishment.' This is exactly what anyone arrogant and insecure enough to consider themselves *part* of an establishment wants you to do. It flatters their sense of having something you want.

    3.1 What do *you* want, anyway? To replace the established order with you and your friends? Real noble aspiration there, nepotism boy.

4. Never write a poem about how great poetry is. As an alternative, try writing a great poem. Use things like imagery, line-break, wit.

    4.1 For instance the following passage does none of the things it says it's going to do: 'Poetry breaks open your skull like a spoon on a boiled egg / Poetry discovers electricity / Poetry is like flying a kite except *you're* the kite.'

5. Most poems about films amount to the poet saying, 'I've seen this film.' Likewise poems about novels, art galleries and music convey less interesting information than a conversation with somebody about any one of the above. This is an artistic inferiority complex. A poem doesn't have to borrow *all* of its substance from another genre.

LUKE KENNARD

5.1 When you have finished your poem, submerge it in ordinary vegetable oil overnight. The next morning use it to roll a cigarette. The poem you write after smoking yesterday's poem will be the true poem

6. Most of your audience share your (and my) vaguely left-wing, vaguely disillusioned politics. Politicians and the heads of industry do not quake when you critique the petroleum industry. It is not just that they haven't heard of you; it is that they *never will*.

6.1 PRACTICAL EXERCISE: Write a pro-war poem.

7. Writing is 90% showing off.

7.1 You have not been 'overlooked' by the Nobel Prize for Literature.

8. Why does *anyone* want to be published? It's like being addicted to getting marks for things, like never leaving school because you need to have everything validated. Mark my marriage! Mark my taste in holidays! Mark my imagination!

8.1 Did I pass? Did I?

GOVERNMENT WARNING
(AUTOMATIC MANIFESTO #6)

for Jackson Mac Low

Poetry may be harmful to your health. It may contain words that appear

nonsensical, contradictory, vague, confusing, upsetting, passionate, naive, sincere, hypocritical, self-absorptive, oppositional, sycophantic, elliptical, discontinuous, cultic, algebraic, glyphic, paranoid, twisted, confessional, professional, paraprofessional, democratic, aesthetic, Platonic, linguistic, simplistic, community conscious, individualistic, autonomous, anarchic, retroactive, reactionary, progressive, primary, secondary, critical, lyrical, disoriented, representational, non-representational, gossipy, sensualistic, archaic, moralizing, hypnotizing, numbing, conclusive, evasive, pitched, cloying, unlicensed, sadistic, egoistic, persuasive, possessive, elusive, elitist, mysterious, malicious, contrite, forgiving, damnable, classic, romantic, futuristic, symbolist, circumstantial, socialist, dubious, capitalist, deconstructive, modern, post-modern, neo-post-modern, neonascent, neurotic, conditional, purist, grammatical, invasive, rapacious, paradoxical, gluttonous, busy, utopian, multicultural, ballistic, pacifist, psychopathic, elevated, primitive, sophisticated, melancholy, disappointing, friendly, effusive, moronic, basic, repetitive, gargantuan, hidden, exhibitionist, European, obvious, literal, found, phenomenal, poisoned, deluded, disregarding, disregarded, marginal, limited, dismissed, sanctioned, cliquish, publicized, modish, old-fashioned, Millennial, pre-Millennial, post-Millennial, turn-of-the-century, spacey, dull, doltish, divisive, puzzling, trapped, theoretical, political, apolitical, postpolitical, moribund, impressionist, sexist, adolescent, unconscious, preconscious, postconscious, neoconscious, paraconscious, conscientious, sloppy, prototypical, blurred, bumbling, lightweight, canonical, official, amateurish, peripheral, ephemeral, Zen, luminous, numinous, lexical, sexist, monogamous, polygamous, polymorphic perverse, angelic, transformative, hippie, psychedelic, agrammatical, disorganized, Aristotelian, teleological, theological, philosophic, lyric, prosaic, versified, monolithic, paralyzing, paralytic, truthful, distorted, pretentious, gibberish, pleading, pleasing, sleazy, punctual, tardy, tendentious, heuristic, permissive, square, deliberate, procedural, complacent, compliant, imitative, wordy, repetitive, simplistic, indeterminate, stolid, traditional, paranormal, enterprising, lewd, inflexible, temporizing, naked, formalist, rejecting, asexual, gossipy, prejudiced, stereotyped, adventurous, collaborative, friendly, warm, inviting, symbiotic, parenthetical, mellifluous, public, private, solipsistic, unstructured, selfish, patronizing, intellectualizing, self-serving, corporate, academic,

NICK PIOMBINO

gratifying, gentle, germinative, fussy, Whitmanesque, Stevensian, Steinian, MLA, quietist, dissonant, noisy, toadying, stylish, dispassionate, objective, found object, deceptive, dolorous, meditative, patriarchal, fascistic, Capitalistic, Marxist, Catholic, bigoted, bullying, pre-emotive, sumptuous, beneficial, depriving, confusing, pointless, ordinary, annoying, lengthy, demeaning, defusing, noncommittal, uncommitted, sequential, delusional, nerdish, schizophrenic, Freudian, worldly, novelistic, plodding, non-narrative, fragmented, sly, sweet, sordid, unfinished, discontinuous, slow, endless, impressionistic, cute, frantic, monopolizing, avoidant, proud, late, lost, limited, hectoring, sadistic, masochistic, cute, demonic, hesitant, trite, torturous, sanctimonious, delightful, different, jaded, piquant, smooth, direct, lucid, light, embittered, agist, promotional, anxious, prepositional, philosophical, fictive, fun, pedagogical, snowed, clichéd, severe, processual, functional, faddish, foppish, bland, corny, transcendent, euphemistic, aphoristic, obnoxious, totalizing, fictive, Neolithic, unlicensed, revelatory, political, commensurate, cognitive, tempting, telepathic, tough, teasing, incomplete, predictable, random, spontaneous, impromptu, tangential, wistful, diluted, condensed, disconnected, tight, torn, wasteful, obscure, oblique, uptight, dirty, controlled, telegraphic, structuralist, surreal, expressionistic, dirty, forgettable, suggestive, arch, sarcastic, melancholy, sneaky, serious, sleepy, bombastic, cool, tense, visual, glum, venerable, lost, listless, lovely, loose, terse, tangential, hopeless, critical, Benjaminian, apt, tongue-in-cheek, experimental, innovative, warped, weird, furious, formless, flawed, flaky, perfect, planned, festive, aching, long, loud, vaporous, vapid, formidable, trashy, depressed, manic, egotistical, bright, normal, creative, boring, wise, campy, special, unique, typical, engaged, voiceless

THE WAR POEM LETTERS

Dear Mr. Kennard,

There follows a transcript of your poem for any corrections you may wish to make before it is cast in bronze by Emily Farraday:

A STATUE OF THE WAR

Statues commissioned during wartime are always controversial—but this one was a life-size bronze cast of the war *as it happened*, covering several hundred square miles, representing the base camps and armoured vehicles and road-blocks in intense detail, right down to flasks of tomato soup and letters from loved ones, all cast in bronze. And it was dropped by cranes right on top of the battle-field itself, squashing flat the soldiers and the police force and the insurgents without discernment.

A Poem by L. N. Kennard

Please return this page to me with corrections added in red ink before the end of the week and we can get on with this exciting project.

Yours faithfully,
Gillian Norrish
ASST. DIR., CREATIVE PARTNERSHIPS

Dear Gillian,

Thank you so much for the letter—I'm really excited to be collaborating with the council on this project; it has got me over several humps in my personal life—about which the less said the better! (internet, gambling). I enclose the corrected proofs. (I haven't made any corrections). Hope you are well.

Yrs sncrly,
Luke

LUKE KENNARD

Dear Mr. Kennard,

We are pleased to announce that your prose poem, 'STATUE OF THE WAR' has been cast in bronze and displayed on a 'broken pillar' statue outside the Magistrates Court. As discussed, we are paying you £5,400 for your services to art and literature. As something of a poet myself, may I take the liberty to say that I enjoyed your piece, but felt that the adjective 'intense' before the word 'detail' to be a little abstract. I say 'a little'; I mean 'a lot'. But I suppose there's not much you can do now that it's cast in bronze, is there?

Yours faithfully,
Gillian Norrish
ASST. DIR., CREATIVE PARTNERSHIPS

Dear Gillian,

Thank you for your criticism—it is a rare treat for me to receive honest opinions about my work: my friends (who I suspect don't understand it anyway) are always really nice—even when I give them a rubbish poem on purpose just to test them. I have even submitted deliberately bad poetry to my publisher at Sane Horse Press—who publishes it without passing a single comment. I have recently started to doubt whether he actually *reads* my work and have written a sonnet which insults him acrostically to check.

It is depressing being a poet. My last book sold 22 copies—(and eighteen of those were to the Creative Writing evening class I teach after I burst into tears in front of them, so they don't really count).

Yeah, I know I should put myself out there more, but the last time I read at a poetry festival I got punched in the mouth afterwards by a performance poet (who recited doggerell about Ann Summers parties and drinking too much which, I might add, got a standing fucking ovation). And I found him on an internet discussion board saying he'll do it again if he ever gets the chance. So you'll appreciate my reluctance to 'hang out' with that crowd.

Dear Dario Jacobs,

I recently discovered that *my own mother* didn't buy a copy of my last book, *Gathering Dust in May* (Sane Horse Press, 2006)—although maybe I should have given her one of the comps.

Listen to me! I'll be pouring my soul out to the debt recovery services next!

I think the sculpture looks brilliant and it has been a great privilege to work with you and Emily. Hope all goes well for you.

Yours,
Luke

Just wanted to write a quick line to thank you for your not entirely disparaging article in the *Argus* today. It is indeed an 'interesting and controversial project', so well done for noticing that and pointing it out.

I've always said that if I wasn't a poet, I'd be a journalist. I have the utmost respect for anyone who can actually get paid for writing things—when those things aren't, say, numbers on a spreadsheet or purchase ledger and that payment isn't £4.45 an hour. (A whole two pounds an hour less than the cleaners whose wage slips I process—not that I have anything against cleaners who actually have to work a lot harder than I do sitting at a desk all day, so don't try to turn this into some kind of class thing).

I think you might have found a more flattering photo than that one of me aged 14 in my swimming trunks at the Heart Disease Swimathon (if you'd asked I would have provided you with one), but thanks for drawing the public attention to my work all the same—poetry needs all the publicity it can get, I think you'll agree!—even if there are several small typographical errors in the reproduction of 'STATUE OF THE WAR' and this article will probably only serve to raise my profile among people who don't like me anyway and awaken my well-burried memories of being picked on at school. You should be proud to call yourself a 'hack'.

Yours,
Luke Kennard

Dear Luke Kennard,

What a waste of my council tax! In fact, what a waste of my time reading your stupid poem! If *you* are considered a poet, I would hate to read something by someone who is *not* considered a poet! If this jokey, smug, self-referential bullshit is what is considered 'creative writing' these days, then I'm proud to call myself uncreative.

Yours,
Nigel Denahy (Poet)

LUKE KENNARD

Dear Mr. Kennard,

I saw your poem, 'A STATUE OF THE WAR' outside the Magistrates Court today and I just wanted to let you know I think it's a load of rubbish. 'Ooh, I've got an MA! Ooh, I've read Borges and can bastardise some of his ideas! Ooh, love me, love me, love me!' That's what it sounded like to me.

Yrs,
His Eminence, Chief Justice Havers

Dear Mr. Kennard,

You may think it's funny to make shit up about something you know nothing about in which lots of people die, but my husband, who died protecting your right to do so in the war you can't seem to bring yourself to take seriously, would doubtless have thought otherwise. In what way, *please* be so kind to tell me, is this half-baked sophistry from an upper-middle-class pansy-boy in the community spirit? Most of the community have some sense of responsibility to each other, even if you so very obviously don't. Whenever I walk past the Magistrate's Court with my daughter I shield her eyes from your atrocity. Kindly remove your so-called 'poem' from outside the Magistrates Court immediately.

In fury,
Elizabeth Rafferty

Dear Ms. Rafferty,

Your letter has humbled me and I am very sorry for your loss. I suppose it was wrong to write about war: it is not something I have ever fought and I conducted no research before writing my poem. Both of my grandfathers would be very disappointed—and you are right to question my masculinity and class-consciousness, which are nascent at best.

I regret that I am unable to remove my poem—which I now hate—as it was commissioned by the council as a creative partnership between me, a bronze caster called Emily Farraday and whoever it was who made the stone pillar. Some guy. And it is supposed to stay there forever. I will try writing to Gillian Norrish—who commissioned the piece, and whose address I can supply if you'd like—and see if I can't get it taken down.

I really want to get it taken it down.

In the mean time, maybe you can take some comfort in the fact that, as you say, your husband died fighting for my right to 'write shit about stuff' and that that is a right I have very much exercised, even if it was only to insult him.

Yours apologetically,
Luke Kennard

Dear Gillian,

How about taking down that stupid poem?

Yrs,
Kennard

Dear Mr. Kennard,

That is out of the question. You have been paid for the poem; we have bought it from you and it belongs to us. As stipulated in the contract —which you were under no obligation to sign if you didn't want to—the piece is set to remain outside the Magistrates Court for a minimum of thirty-nine years; which will almost certainly be the remainder of yours and my lives—and there is not a thing to be done about that, I'm afraid.

Yours faithfully,

Gillian Norrish
Asst. Dir., Creative Partnerships

Dear Mr. Kennard,

I take no comfort in your letter whatsoever. Actions speak louder than words and the only words I would find comforting would be words uttered with sufficient force to knock down your so-called 'poem' and blow it away —and it is made of bronze, so that isn't very likely ever to happen, even if the big bad wolf himself huffed and puffed and blew it down.

It may interest you to know that I am organising a protest and a petition against your 'poem' and have so far gathered no less than eighty-three signatures—and that was without even trying, really. You are going down, Kennard, so try to sleep while you are worrying about that all the night long.

Elizabeth Rafferty

Dear Ms. Rafferty,

Perhaps I didn't make myself clear: I too hate my poem. Please forward me the petition and I will be more than happy to add my own signature.

Yrs,
Kennard

P.S. I am, of course, an insomniac, so your attempts to terrorise me amount to spitting in the ocean.

Gillian,

LUKE KENNARD

I really think you should consider taking the poem down. I've received several letters of complaint and have already offered to write a new, better poem which wouldn't offend those who are only trying to protect me from the threat of terrorism and who have given up their own, brilliant lives so that I can live my own, stupid one in peace and without being killed for reasons I don't even understand. Maybe I could write a poem about *that*. What do you think? A *pro*-war poem — what could be more radical than that? In an age where the organisers of anti-war coalitions take home six-figure sallaries and Christmas bonuses — when Christmas is the very thing the war is being fought about, as far as I can see. Disgusting. Whaddayasay, Gillian? Huh? How about it?

It makes me weep to think that I have contributed to the status-quo of 'war-bashing' while people like Elizabeth Rafferty were losing their loved ones. Please, please, please take the poem down. I haven't spent all of the money yet and could probably still afford to pay Emily Farraday to cast the new poem in bronze. Can I send you some drafts? Please say yes.

In desperation,
Kennard

LUKE KENNARD

Dear Mr. Kennard,

The tone of your last letter was quite frenzied. I recommend that you spend some of the fee you received for your perfectly innoccuous little poem taking a long holiday somewhere far away from here until this blows over. I myself am going on holiday tomorrow, so please do not write to me at this address for a fortnight.

Yours faithfully,

Gillian Norrish
Asst. Dir., Creative Partnerships

Dear Sir,

Further to the recent slew of letters pertaining to my poem 'STATUE OF THE WAR', I would like to add that the poem is not only 'disrespectful', 'weird', 'not very good', 'a waste of money', 'hypocritical' and 'stupid', but also a craven piece of careerist maneuvering. You see, I care far more about impressing the right people and trying to claw myself into some position of influence within the 'world' of 'poetry' than I do about writing poetry itself— which means I am a charlatan.

If you ever see me eating anything, you should wrest it from my hands and throw it to a dog. I am not fit to walk on the same streets as the rest of you and so have taken to walking in the gutter. You'll recognise me because I will be wearing a bobble hat, even though it is summer. I guess that's the kind of obtrusively 'wacky' guy I am.

Sin Cellery (Ha ha! I'm a language poet!),
Luke Kennard, MA

Dear Miss Farraday,

I don't really know who else to turn to. I so enjoyed working with you on our project and felt that we had a connection; words and bronze are really not so different when you look at it metaphorically.

The first sign that something is wrong in my life is always that I have stopped reading the *London Review of Books* and am just putting it under things instead. This morning I found *eight London Reviews of Books* under a vase. I have been eating only Pringles. Whenever I am not eating Pringles, my stomach hurts until I eat more. I haven't written a single thing—apart from lots of letters—since the painful thing started.

I hope that this whole miserable turn of events has not had the same effect on you and that you are not greeted every morning by a stack of hate-mail. Maybe you would like to meet for a drink some time to discuss future collaborations? I am free every day and night.

Yrs,
Luke

Dear Luke,

It's *Mrs.* Farraday, actually, and thank you for your very kind letter. Don't take all of this so hard—Wittgenstein wrote his thesis in the trenches! Stay strong!

Love,
Emily
x

LUKE KENNARD

Dear Emily,

Is making reference to another man's bravery in the face of *actual war* supposed to make me feel better? Because it doesn't. In fact it's more than a little insensitive. I guess the things they say about people who work with resistant materials are true: that you are insensitive.

Yrs,
Luke

Dear Gillian,

I'm assuming you've returned as it has been precisely two weeks since you left for your 'holiday'—although I might add that I distinctly saw your car outside the council offices last Tuesday and it was gone that same night. Maybe you were lending it to someone else—because that's something that people do all the time, isn't it? Lending one another their cars. (You do understand sarcasm, don't you, Gillian?)

Anyway, I'm writing to say I no longer care what happens. I'm resigned to being a pariah for the rest of my life. I hope you feel guilty for making a poet's self-esteem lower—which is somewhat akin to making a drowning dog wetter.

I could have loved you, Gillian.

Yrs,
Luke N. Kennard, (PhD pending)

Dear Mr. Kennard,

We write to inform you that Ms. Norrish is no longer employed by the Creative Partnership's department. She left instructions only to reveal her forwarding address to *craftspeople* and to tell the *artists* she worked with over the years that it had been 'a blast' and wish you every luck in the future.

Yours sincerely,

Robert Talmage
DIR. INCUMBENT, CREATIVE PARTNERSHIPS

Dear Stephen,

Please find attached my new manuscript, *The War Poem Letters*, which, being my sixth collection in as many godforsaken years, should fulfill my contract with all of you at Sane Horse Press. *The War Poem Letters* is only twenty pages long, but as it is *prose poetry* and not *poetry*, it contains about a hundred times more words than most of the so called 'books' that you 'publish' anyway—even the really long ones like that wannabe Charles Olsson reject _____ _____ who seems to be averaging about half a fucking PUNCTUATION MARK a page these days. God damn the whole poetry 'world' and everyone in it.

Maybe you could add a foreword saying words to that effect. If not, I suppose we could spread every poem over three pages and put in a dozen blanks at the back for notes or something—or maybe just repeat those twenty pages three times; that should save the printers from struggling with an inadequate page-count for a perfect bound spine. You are still *doing* perfect bound spines, aren't you, Stephen? Because if you're not, I'm totally sending this manuscript elsewhere. To Harold at Blindside, for instance. Also the managing

LUKE KENNARD

editor at Glass & Glassman once patted me on
the back at a conference, so I'd watch out if I
were you—you could be losing 'the most un-
derrated writer of his—or, indeed, any other
—generation.' —*Sane Horse Magazine*.

Threateningly,
Kennard

LA BELLE DAME SANS MATRIX

in memoriam

Agent Smith is crouching down to Sylvia Plath. She is strapped
to a chair with black & red typewriter ribbons. Her hands

are free in her lap, but her mouth
is gagged. Sylvia's eyes stare defiance,

cold but on fire, as Smith begins,

for the 9th time, his interrogation. He loosens
the knot of his black tie, takes away his black shades, disconnects

the curly transparent worm whispering
in his ear. Now Smith's lower lip pouts as his words curl

slowly out from his mouth, to wriggle
in amongst the mass of cells that're Plath's brain:

'So, at last, the great Sylvia Plath. I have her gagged! Perhaps,
Miss Plath you'd like to type WHY there is still this incessant

stink in here with us. In my nostrils, Miss Plath, this . . . this
inescapable smell. Why? Is it sweat, the foul animal aroma

of Sex, Miss Plath? Or perhaps it is the stench of Death?
My colleagues think I'm wasting my time with you,

but I think you want to do the write thing.' Agent Smith slides
a table & typewriter across the room using his mind, and stops.

MARK GOODWIN

It just in front of Sylvia's fingers. The keys glisten. She begins
to reach, but there is a dragging-screech

as Smith's mind slides the table away
                                        one imperial American inch.

Dear Reader, now adjust your viewpoint through
many points in a single circumference around

Sylvia strapped & gagged but reaching fast
for her typewriter. See her high-speed

flinch for the keys slowed
in an ooze of time. Through her nose Sylvia breathes

in and the ink-ridden straps across her chest slowly snap; hear
the twang of each breaking fibre as she grabs

for her alph a bet & sacred vowels, her fingers hissing
as air-molecules slip along the grooves of her fingerprints.

And now the paper in the typewriter is reeling
at miles an hour, but you, Reader, can see,

milliseconds delayed to nearly a minute, as her fingers
punch the code: connect, connect to spread

her deadly pattern of black ink across a blank
rectangular section called A4. It infects, it breeds. Smith reads:

'You don't do, Baddy, you Simulated Agent, you.
You're not even a you. But I'm an i, the i in Die.

You met Me in the meadow of a memory. My fat
gold heart slaps against my lungs pulling in men.

And there is a charge, a very large charge, to watch
a woman undress her bones until perfected: black

sweet mouthfuls of shadows, the blood of words.'

Sylvia has ripped out the gag and so begins
to take in one long lung-filling breath. The wOman

is inspired. Her purpose rushes, pumping through her.

Angel Smith's mouth is gaping black & wide, he is pale,
and on his brow there're drops of illuminated dew. He wails

vowels as now

Plath's black rain of letters splatters through his brain. Tears
are rolling like molten silver down Smith's cheeks. Just

for an instant, just before deletion, just as he's passing
through Plath's naked mouth, Agent Smith finally feels,

finely feels what it's like to be real.

MARK GOODWIN

the idea

as word
the idea
sound

the idea
as thought
thought

as word
the sound
idea

the word
as sound
thought

as idea
the thought
sound

the sound
as word
word

as thought
& sound
thought

word
as idea &
the word

the word

just as i start

this
believing a
few mere lines

might alter every
thing—so it
is

that
look you
glance me as you

dance from bath
to drawer
can

open
my mouth
rock this tongue

to some sure
thing i all
but

say

POETRY FINDS STATIC

(A Manifesto)

Poetry rides shotgun on a highway going nowhere anyhow. Let's just get that straight out front. You just want to find a station. Let's get that straight too. I can't remember the last time poetry put in. It can tell a story. That is true. But it's no friend. Don't make that mistake. Sometimes poetry shakes you to wake you. That is true. Poetry always turns to the station you don't want to hear no how. Is that true? Poetry never finds it anyway. It gets stuck between stations. Poetry finds static. You can almost hear what it's trying to say. That is true. But it can drive you mad. That is true too. Two tunes at once. Can poetry be both? What isn't really? That might be true. Poetry takes its time or no time. Depending. What is poetry but language? What is language but the scenery? The same images shifting perception, each of us interpreting but not really knowing. As if you could. As if it could. What is true? If nothing else, that is. It makes sense to look at poetry this way and that. Drip comes close. Buzz is closer, but that's about it. Whisper and sizzle and clang too I guess. There are more of course, but no more are needed. Buzz Whisper Sizzle Drip Clang. Drip Whisper Clang Buzz Sizzle. How can that be true? No, true, of course, is meadow horse lake love nightingale God. So true yet it certainly doesn't seem so. The road is what we decide. Get that straight if nothing. Poetry finds static.

Gertrude Stein said there ain't no answer. She also said there ain't gonna be an answer and there never has been an answer. That, she said, is the answer. Poetry is as good an answer as any. Or not. If poetry claims to have the answer it is lying maybe. Maybe not. How do you know? Gertrude Stein says so, that's how. Poetry finds static. That is the only true thing. Poetry will smoke your last cigarette. It sits beside you or behind you. It sleeps a lot. Poetry can be ahead of you sometimes always anyway. That may be true or not. Don't ever let poetry drive. For that you'll be sorry. If you only take one thing away from this or that let it be. Poetry is not dependable. It barely looks at the road ahead anyway. It gawks at the rabbits and the tumbleweeds and the lines behind. It will leave you in the ditch or worse. That is true. Out of gas and out of cash listening to static. Believe it or don't—it doesn't matter much anyway. An old, drunk poet said there are worse things than being alone. That may be true. But he didn't say what. He also said that friendship means sharing the prejudice of experience. That of everything seems true. So maybe poetry is your friend. Remember, it can tell a good story if you let it. You can let it. But you have to be willing to listen to both stations at once.

MICHAEL KERR

OUR INNER PEACE IS EARTH'S FRONTIER

(Good Advice For Some Young Poets)

MICHAEL MOLYNEUX

Poetry should hit
at once like a train passing through the
    dense night
and like a quiet dawn benediction.
It must be honest and speak with
    awareness, and a voice
that is familiar to everyone but which has
    never been heard;
Poetry is a force of nature,
the poet is a force of nature;
The true poetry is not written in ink, in
    clever words or syntax,
it does not resemble an antique that has
    been repaired with bits of old plastic,
and yet so many of us strive merely for
    cathartic glory
and try to pass off our sorrow as art;
No! the true poetry is written in branches
    and in veins,
in river deltas that somehow weep and
    moan through us,
it is our job to remain pure to the task of
    listening to those cries,
and to drain off our self-interest,
so that we might better perform our duty,
clearing a passage in our hearts
through which the world's heavy distillate
    might flow;
gradually broadening the mysterious voice
    of the self-conscious earth

that tries to listen to itself
above the clamorous machinery
of our egos.

STRATEGIES

How tired Sutton is of writers. Yet he never passes a bookshop without entering.

And so a thick fugginess descends. Yes I'm referencing Orwell's essay—Sutton is one of those fish-like creatures. Something demersal and nudging through mud.

Only I know the hatred refluxing inside, slipping through the over-praised volumes by authors in profile who 'write like angels'.

For the worst he saves his tearing and insertion of cat shit. One in particular has him gouging with rage.

Inescapable this bastard. At 3.18 p.m. on a drop-away Wednesday in March . . . there he is, preening in the Arts section of a broadsheet. Adding to the irritation, we're reading it in the Costa Coffee shop at Basingstoke station.

'. . . at these times, poetry finds a way to speak. Maybe a lone voice in the gale, which can steer us through the maelstrom and offer us shelter. In my public role, I too struggle to find a space, where the words can sing and coalesce. That's why I've called my new collection 'Scott's Bivouac'. I'm sure we can all picture it—the polar vastness, the huddled bodies under sagging canvas. But what do we remember most? I suggest it's the few words he scribbled to us—to posterity . . .'

This idiot's career has been carefully fabricated, assisted by a blizzard of cronies. His most famous poem is a graceless and unac-knowledging raid on Kipling's 'Without Benefit of Clergy'.

So another Orwell reference. Our heroes get exfoliated by writers we hate.

Well, I've decided to strike back. In what mustn't appear a concerted campaign, we'll flay and expose these popinjays.

Me and Sutton—my guide and executor.

1. HOW TO MEET THE POET

He frequently travels from London to the provinces—his term, used 'ironically' (but still used).

Often by train; though if possible taxi—once a round trip to Sheffield and back, handing the festival organizers the bill (he read for twenty minutes).

If attempting to locate on a train, look in first class. Although you could try listening outside the toilet cubicles—he sometimes receives noisy felatio from one of his creative writing students, yelling the penultimate verse from 'La Belle Dame Sans Merci' on ejaculating.

But seriously, I enrolled for his course. Sent off my stuff then came across as wistful and focussed at the interview. And quoted from his work.

PAUL SUTTON

2. HOW TO PUBLISH A COLLECTION

How's life been so far? I'm guessing comfortable. Even if you claim a struggle through sink-estates and gender discrimination—that's all for the pulpit.

But for some reason people listen. So I'd like to ask—Su Tenderdrake / Jed Bracewell / Tilly Greenslade / Mebhan name in Irish—why none of you are ugly?

Where does your liberalism come from? I suggest self-satisfied hugging, as you watch scuttlers collecting trolleys or working as usherettes.

As for the collection—no one buys them, so its purpose is existential.

But I'm sure to finger it—testing the binding for loose pages, tugging 'til they give.

Maybe scrawling a racist message and signing in your name.

3. HOW TO WALK INTO A ROOM

Why are you always apologizing? You've the same right to pavement as the next; more than some marauder who hopped over from Kurdistan to drive mini-cabs in Stoke Newington. Or Albanians who have liberals foaming in sympathy—placards outside Campsfield, candle vigils at Carfax.

Did we need more pimps and pushers? Don't mention that their treatment of women isn't quite suited to the Society section of *The Guardian.*

Careful. I wonder if you've seen the ice cliff, compacted and blue, shuddering over your head. It collapses at the onset of screeching from the broadsheet gallery—and they never rest. I feel them sniffing the air for you.

Remember your first encounter? Your voice was dry; they knew your weakness in being right.

Tenderdrake has destroyed lesser opponents than this. When she knows your presence, the stare arrives; so does the drill-bit in her voice.

'I'm finding this offensive.'

She's not in the least offended—never has been. Once, a ghost of a 19th Century chamber maid (rogered and discarded by that purple cad upstairs) happened on Tenderdrake bullying a check-out girl in Tesco's.

The poor ghost fainted to think her suffering had produced only this!

If only it were true.

4. HOW TO WRITE WHEN YOU CAN'T SPEAK

Familiar the landfill of your dialogue with seagulls strutting over its mounds so no end to what you'll say given which the idea of your writing is terrifying and I can only hide head under pillow where the typing still reaches me and I have to emerge when my ears get too hot and you've by then finished a first novel based on a slave ship and a family saga with colonial angst and fake reconciliation why when people imagine themselves backwards do they never feature as the villains I mean someone did those things which they showboat themselves opposing.

5. HOW TO WAIT

This isn't a gift.

Make a study of people waiting—in boredom doeth man showeth his true natuyre.
Look occupied. The slow hush of earnest activity. In essence, there is office fodder.
But above the beasted level, a few rise and assume authority; speaking in languor.

How delightful their downfall, floundering
    for the rope—I hold it back;
flick it toward them for teasing then throw
    it down the well.
Astonishing how ugly the English can be—
    angular and surely
built for buggery. Now has arisen a
    grasping elite
who understandeth not cites and,
    hopefully, await

mugging or dealers moving into their
    street.

I imagine sitting out the winter in suphur
    smog,
seeing my hated neighbours dissolve,
    praying not
to hear their footsteps return. But in any
    season,
such as these survive—acquiring, nesting,
    plotting.

6. HOW TO GAIN ACCEPTANCE

You have one of those translucent natures.
Your disdain and hate show like bad skin
through a face with too much make-up.
I'm unconvinced you're worth inviting to
    my house,
listening to the maybe essential
    exaggerations;
even Christmas can't disguise your lack of
    purpose.
But maybe we can be friends, I need to
    rebuild myself
through degrading and chastening failure.

7. HOW TO APPROACH A TABLE OF ENEMIES

Ascertain their number. Before opening the door, decide who to fix on. No doubt their con-

PAUL SUTTON

versation will drop when you approach. Be aware of the sideways glances but don't move from face to face. Allow the fact of your presence to become unassailable. The one you stare at should be the weakest.

Avoid Scots—not just now, but always. They suffer more outbreaks of e-coli than's healthy.

Too busy hating the English, they forget to wash their hands after wiping.

Sit down and stare.

8. HOW TO LEAVE

Walk straight and get up before breathing in.

9. HOW TO LET THEM KNOW YOU KNOW THEY KNOW

Perhaps they don't; but for our purposes, assume so.

Build something permanent—maybe a shopping complex in an old canal basin, or a nightclub on an implausible stretch of dual carriageway.

One day they'll visit.

10. HOW TO WRITE LIKE AN ANGEL WITHOUT DANCING ON THE HEAD OF A PIN

Difficult. I could labour the point that there's been little if anything published by harp play-

ers with wings. Instead I undertake a systematic re-formatting of my life. Having always suffered from a coruscating (not simpering) cynicism, I soon find myself friendless when I start beaming optimistically and talking about opportunities. Never mind. My reward will come.

The other problem is I dislike most people, and they feel the same about me. My physical presence can cause outrage—a fevered emanation seems to infuriate even passing motorists.

My self-help book on becoming a success was called 'Stop being a jerk'. It sold three million copies.

AN EXTRACT:

'Ever been stuck on a train, in a traffic jam, at an airport? Of course. Next time take a look around. Sure, most people are fuming, muttering obscenities, suffering and causing stress.

Not me. I'm the one in the corner, fingers buzzing over my lap-top. Because I use my time. I don't let anybody else. Not leaves on the line, suicidal leapers or French air-traffic controllers.

Get into the habit of owning time. It's something all of us successful people do.

I have a tip to share. Get up now and go to the bathroom. Listen. In one of the cubicles will be a fellow employee, pretending to take a dump but actually reading the paper. Find out who it is. That sort of information can be dynamite when your organisation starts to down-size.

Whatever you do, make yourself the master. I don't care if you're the MD of a blue-chip or the guy serving fries. Be the master. Show me you care.

Because I do.'

MANIFESTO

PAUL TAYLOR

trombonepoetry
revives bardic
outlandishness
making poems a
bebop blow-out
outstripping a
normal limping
expressionless
performance of
obscurantic or
effete blather
turning tables
realigning the
yesterday mind

trombonepoetry
ransacks books
of melodies to
merge modes in
bacchic blasts
of celebration
navigating new
expanses every
poem a mapping
of possibility
every invented
tune an argosy
re-jigged as a
yacht of words

trombonepoetry
revels in curt
obsequent free
music suddenly
billowing into
otherwise dull
nights hearing
endless verses
purportedly in
oracular style
except for the
troubling fact
rows of people
yawn endlessly

trombonepoetry
reaches for an
opportunity to
mix sounds and
bring together
online or live
new poems plus
extemporary or
prepared music
opening up the
exploration of
thelonious art
rebetika riffs
yardbird songs

trombonepoetry
relishes music
owlishly hoots
melancholy and
brass brazenly
open heartedly
newly mintedly
evergreeningly
plays on poems
of indigo mood
ellingtoning a
tale of hunger
reconstructing
younger tempos

trombonepoetry
riffs and rags
overtones with
muted meanings
broadside digs
or hatchet job
neatly beating
esoteric fancy
poultry geists
on broken eggs
excavating all
the numbskulls
rattling dusty
yarns to beats

TECHNIQUE COMES HARD

Technique comes hard. Staying the course. Alcohol eases. Nuttall said you can avoid all these issues by staying high ah the blur the power the fog. We were in the bar and should have been on stage. Nuttall's stage. Lunge at the microphone like a maypoll. Wet mouth open mouth like Louis Zukofsky hard mouth like Raoul Hausmann Welsh mouth like Dylan Thomas. Poem bug pom pim. Got this got this. Papur doesn't matter. Spit. Shower. Hold hold God damn.

Nuttall said walk hell walk they want you to read poems give em a novel give them fiction stream of consciousness can't tell the beginning from the end like Warhol's Empire State was it the Empire State culture of the bomb all they want is that—time's gone by new stuff next. They ask these old bluesharp revivalist guitar pickers found on stoops out in the back of dust southern states well what was it like in 1936 in that studio shack south of the tracks when you were up front and who played behind you was it Shaking Hard Arm or Blind Blake on bass? Guy doesn't know all he wants to hear is how it was today what he's laid down just now those twelve bars has he still got it? Tell me tell me. Willie McTell could have done that better. Son House and ole Ashbery certainly did.

Met X at the bus station driven here from the European iron east welcome to the south

Wales drizzle still old world but light in the skies. Haversack full of pubs. These for review put them in the mag. Second Aeon that was once part of my life. These are tape boxes once held 7″ reels of Scotch. One full of shaving foam and an oily bolt. One cutupbits unspliced rattles. One little mimeo products and a book of matches. One with battery and balloon (uninflate) one with matches and balloon (deflate) some ink cake mix and Bible fragments threads watch dial parts of loaf immersed in paint vinyl holding shape like landscape of the Herefordshire fields. Recalls Nuttall. I say this.

We stack them. Ideas. Put them in a bucket to get echo. Get the drums from tapping the side of the booth and the edge of the chair. Flared trousers. Big haircuts. Oxfam jackets. Drink takes the edge. Somewhere it comes together Jeff told me that.

In the new world the past is invisible. Nuttall vanished. Poems impossible to get. View is a year no one looks further back than that. Discover what's already been discovered. Invent again what's been invented. Say you are new. Wave a flag. Nuttall and a cornet bottom of the garden. The bombers fly, dark shapes in the dark sky. Lunge again at the microphone. Tell them. They won't know they don't know the past either. Tell them you've told them. Tell them again.

ADVICE TO A YOUNG WRITER

I

It is very easy:
It is very easy to be
Told a narrative of elegance.
Everybody likes to pay for it.
This is one,
Any after effect is pleasant.

II

We will now find out what sentences are.
Think of how they do not wear cuff-buttons.
A sentence is this. A sentence should be
Thought of as having been told; if you try
To make a sentence lie where it has been put
it stays.
Now make a sentence all alone.

III

A darling dog:
Is that a feeling or an expression?
I wish I knew how I did it,
I have practiced.
A narrative is at present not necessary,
Marshes are preferred to a river.

IV

The part that grammar plays.
Grammar does not play a part:
Forget grammar and think about potatoes.
Do you see?
Grammar in relation to a tree and two horses!
Think of that!

V

Think of a use for a paragraph.
This is a paragraph:
George is wonderfully well,
He has had his portrait painted by
A Frenchman
An Englishman
A Dutchman
And an American.
He looks like his brother.
So far there is no need for a paragraph.

VI

Now to come to something more difficult:
Forensics.
What is forensics?
Forensics is eloquence and reduction;
Forensics are elaborated argument.
A title is made for defence.
Forensics are the words which they like;
Forensics are double.
Have you come in?
Yes I have but I am not in which is a pity.

AUTOMATIC MANIFESTO #7

How hard should I be willing to work to cause the machine to move? Certainly there must be a mode whereby whispering could be amplified into a question of pitch. In this instance, acoustics take off from where the lighting particularly goes dim, a valve which functions like a sprocket and a French Horn, in which arpeggios are frozen by an excess of pain, and melancholy takes on a majestic air. All along it had encompassed the invention of algebra by means of speculative ceramics, hardening a concept into a concerto, filing it carefully under the heading of cataclysm, shortening its attitudinal vowels by means of expanding its preposterous assumptions, which themselves are gradually approaching taciturnity, turning its back on morally absent overtones, shadowing its suspect grammar in the far-off glittering beams of empty supposition which glides gently and slowly into the waiting arms of abstraction, whose speculative hypothetical attractions will never be sufficiently quantified or even humorous despite the ulterior motives of the manifest dream content, sliding its negative transference like a trombone, emptying its confessional syndromes into a grateful interpretation whose arms grotesquely imagine the canon, a broad crypt for encryption's silky significance, permanently imprinted on the broad brows of history. In this context interruption's arms set around it like a gossamer dress, whose limbs entwine even the coldest heart in any probable reality, whose guilts can be tested by ear on the piano of solitude's tones in the cool hands of the precious parenthetical.

Entrusting the whole future of humanity in a complete dependence on words, language's bid for power quietly encircled the heart, blending expression with the unraveled and the unintended in an involuntary inquisition. In any case, it is all a matter of breath, trying to run an adjectival or metaphorical marathon across previously uncomplicated categories which range themselves absently like comedians whose comprehension is ninety-nine parts dogged will and one bright carnation of a thought which plays its grainy rondos on a black and white t.v., in matte soft sleep, airing its tiny representatives in privilege and common law. In a sense, insight as a form of kind rationalism is no defense against heretical and hedonistic philandering or the pillaging inherent in the ravages of bigotry and hate. The more hate the less love, the more love the less hate, with one exception. Those who find hate to be a kind of terrorist and psychopathic glee are orphaned on the forces of castration anxiety and materialistic greed. Forever will they rip holes in the fab-

ric of restful repose and slightly sarcastic conversation, in the late afternoon of a carniva-
lesque and boisterous reconfiguration, vig-
orous, vainglorious, anticipatory, atonal and
abrupt.

A VOICE WITHOUT

To say and not say at
the same time, or

at a different time to not
say and yet say—

eversaying, yes-
saying, gainsaying,

truthsaying, lying,
neversaying so that it

closes into what has been
said; to say that I

am not saying, to not
say that I am not

saying, or at a
different time to say that

has been said, but *this*
will never be said, quite

simply, quite inexplicably,
has never been nor gone,

has arrived without arriving
at what has been, has left

without leaving what is known,
disappears into the unknown

which is left behind, as
never before, said.

NOT ANOTHER POEM

after Krzysztof Ziarek

ROBERT SHEPPARD

Often I am permitted to return to a field. And it is full of forces

Something is happening here, saying whatever, but saying all the same. But not. The same there's nothing to exchange. No need to

Forces don't build in power. Or domination. A thoughtful, forceful relinquishing

Inside this field you are safe but not safe. All that is the world is not. The world. A bullet flies as the idea of a bullet (flies) but its trajectory is turned. To words like 'sleet' turning to 'snow'. To slow. It is a bullet that stands. In relation to every new thing

Everything here is transformed, every thing (out there) interrupted. A snow-bullet frozen mid-air becomes off-centre of a new constellation from where we see it transfigured our selves. What we think of it is the new thing

There's more of it. And more and more of it in a different way there's nothing. We can do with what we find here. It's not stock. This is where. I want to make some thing. Something elsed, but disavowed—disallowed, even—in this

A carafe, That Is a blue guitar. Beyonding art

I don't want to only make relations. I make. The gangly girl in black-framed glasses in my making. I make her trip back from her car to number 99 in her strappy party shoes to root out the Christmas present she has forgotten. Then I will make the thoughts she has as she returns

Outside of her there is domination. House numbers telephone wires. Humming with Power. Not poetry and the antinomies. Satellite navigation. Data shadow. Inside. They share the world is not escaped, but elsed

Empower me to be. So unpowered. In my relinquishment by distance not elevation to keep the saying unsaid. To speak against is to speak. Let me do it I need to do it but let me speak something elsed. From somewhere else. Of something

I have *made* something. For you. Now you are someone else

THE CITY OF CHERISHED WORDS

In the Avenue Sallighazal, poets inscribe interpretations
of each tree's voice on the green pages of its leaves,
so that we can walk through their shushing sighing rhymes
pausing to allow inky lines to ripple kisses over our faces.
Our lips then, are like willow leaves, grown long and slender,
mobile with our breath and Willow's thought.

Poets have business here, moving in their roles
between counsellor, raconteur, seer, priest,
writing whole philosophies in quatrains across
the sanctuaries and dance halls round the Square
or placing motif stories in free verse on the high bleached walls
of the apartments above the trading rooms; these myths
all have a cursive, quickening language,
a new skin's shine for each season.
Sometimes, the calligraphy and phrasing of the latest poem
attracts crowds who stand reading for hours,
murmuring decipherment in eagerness and curiosity
until the rains sweep the wall's white slate clean again
and there is pause for thought.

Of course there is sometimes trouble when visitors misread,
imagine insults in a text without that intent.
They cry out with indignation, wail loudly, berate the authors
as they call to the rainmakers to come quickly
But instead, a poet will take them gently into a grove
and patiently re-write the offending script
on dampened ochre tablets, until the stranger sees
that truths exists even in the rubrics of a different dialect:
what is here, is only a further translation
of the multilingual tongues of love.

There are so many ways to understand.
Up on the hill, one wide-girthed oak is ringed by a seat
of meshed hazel and here the Old come to contemplate the town,
taking in vistas and the conundrums of traffic,
or the growing and fading and going of all who process.
As they listen to messages that oaks or spires or smoke give them
the Old write on dry lozenges of whitegrass parchment
then hang their fluttering responses like moths on the lowest leaves.
These will last the season until Fall allows them to fade,
whispering themselves into earth. Sometimes it is possible
to read them even as they are eaten into filigree by the oak-bugs,
letters becoming the angles of structure, primal language.

Later the fattened insects co-join with the tree,
so new wisdoms are assimilated: memories of bone and blood
notched into branches, history hatched into new wings.

All writers take their work seriously, with full responsibility.
Each strives to find a gift that will grace the mind,
grow like an apple, full of orchards and galaxies
and further generations of thought. Working together,
each month six writers choose a single word to be illuminated
and placed on the skyline for a while,
a starry neon shaping of a meditation such as *leopard*.
Later they may add others, choosing secretive locations
like the underarch of a bridge or the footstone of a house:
feather, grief, pattern. Children love this as a game,
collecting the words like tokens of power.
You see them dancing out their versions on the Sandbook
at low tide, their small heels spinning shells glitter

and spark in the triumph of scribbled phrases that the sea
licks up with other offerings: lotus, incense, recitation.

Water and trees are our spirit,
the wind and the light within them our energy.
We shape ourselves round what is, building the star of our living
to hold three rivers that ribbon the city with lilies and granite.
Where they meet, the divine solace of water flows
through prayers set in stone. This ancient carving is so worn now
that few can read the words yet we have them all by heart;
each day the water sings them and we cherish them
as we do the lifeblood that rivers through our veins
and the pulse that pulls our sun through the smallest atom.

Of course we have Gleaners, who collect, etch, copy.
We have Libraries storing batskins, rolled parchments,
powdery papyrus in glass cases, we keep numbered films,
silver discs, books. But words are the air
and we breathe them into our memories:
always telling us beauty, always telling us life.
So much to praise! Finding the voices of icefields and lions,
the voices of gold and thunder and grit, daylight and dark.
And the dreams—just the dreams! It is endless. There is so much
it can never all be said! Thoughts all fold into each other,
such mouth-music, mind-music, *look*, *listen*, *think*, *feel*, *grow*.
And the people vie with each other to make more joys and glories
for the poets to sing back to them—here, a rapturous birth,
there, a blossoming garden of jasmine and fig; or perhaps
a fresh charm of mathematics, a new treatise on Saturn's phases,
or a good, open-eyed death. All this, even before the questioning.

THE 12 LAWS OF CELESTIAL
& POETICAL MECHANICS

for Peter Dent

RUPERT LOYDELL

1. Shift a few inches to the right. This is not self expression.

2. Get your facts straight. Only lies come close to reality.

3. Inhabit the murky middle not the happy ending. It is crazy not to celebrate whatever reconciles us to life.

4. Know the world as distinct from and outside yourself. It is physically confusing and chaotic, but emotionally consummate.

5. Crave eternal spring. Walk high on the grassy banks.

6. Study single objects. Geometric shapes are not necessarily clear.

7. Make the absent present. Enchantments and every imaginable sort of uncanniness abound.

8. Expose yourself to guilty intention. We do not have to guess at the nature of destruction.

9. Draw some general conclusions. Sense the smallness and quirkiness of the world.

10. Give up everything to be here. Memories may return without the fragrance of familiarity.

11. Set up structures only to collapse them. Lovers of wisdom should enquire into many things.

12. Pay the sum demanded. There is a certain courage involved.

A POEM'S NOT FOR PEOPLE

a poem's not for people
who are afraid the sun won't rise tomorrow
who can help themselves but choose not to
who think giving advice is beneath them
who know the what but not the why

a poem's not for people
who are in a hurry to get a job
who want to work from home
who want their entertainment predictable
who hope their hotel room comes with an in-
    ternet connection

a poem's not for people
who are easily dissuaded or discouraged
who can't follow a running gag
who pick and choose which laws they obey
who need to have simple answers

a poem's not for people
who pay attention to television
who have merely expressed an interest
who are easily offended
who giggle every time they see naked breasts

a poem's not for people who have never con-
    templated Helen of Troy
and wondered at a face that could launch a
    thousand ships

a poem's not for people
with queasy stomachs
with memory loss
with no attention span
with plans for the future
with guns in their homes

a poem's not for people
who won't accept their responsibility to
    analyze and understand

a poem's not for people
who sleep too much
who don't have a social life
who don't know what they want to do
who want to make other people do the
    same things

a poem's not for people
with nothing better to do

a poem's not for people
who can provide visions to order
who want to know who they were in a past
    life
who simply want to avoid hell and gain
    heaven instead
who are looking for special effects and
    bombs bursting in the ear

RUPERT LOYDELL

a poem's not for people
who don't like subtitles or weirdness
who are tired of spending half their lives
      in gridlock
who can't have an intelligent conversation
who are a burden and a threat
who are just passing through
who never do anything wrong
who are trying to cooperate
who know there is more to give
who are afraid of the dark

a poem's not for people
who don't like bone-rattlingly loud music
who like their songs to clock in under
      seven minutes
who aren't in the orchestra
who have two left feet
who dabble in the field
who take such things seriously

a poem's not for people
who are used to seeing somebody die
      before their eyes
who are mindless drones locked up in an
      artificial reality
who cannot stand being crowded or
      uncomfortable
who can't abide the idea of someone
      sleeping in their bed
who want big families with lots of kids

who are thinking about doing some
      project but have not yet started it
who think they have everything right and
      need nothing else
who say they haven't the time to learn

a poem's not for people who can't find
      their way blindfold

THE LAPSED READER
(AUTOMATIC MANIFESTO #8)

He or she will not appear to be utopian. Body can be embarrassing, can 'throw' you.

The thinking mechanism is thrown aside. Reading rises and falls, like waves. It is given over.

It is constantly bursting into existence, birthing. Early on, we can ignore, forget the waiting. Now we can only long for our next chance.

Standing, the young ones lurch. Reading is waiting, forestalling, the prime-pumping that regulates the incorporation. In that sense, at least, it partakes of the body. Reading can do no other than embrace and be embraced. There is ever more to be understood as analogous to the body. Reading gathers, compares, accepts, examines, demands acceptance and accompaniment. It is and demands company, exchange. In doing so, it almost implies submission, at least immersion, thus the cult of skepticism and irony. We can't both submit and be ourselves at the same time. The words reach out like tiny gloved hands on the branches, pianists, organists, soloists. Also, like the body, the reader's text is ever faithfully there. If it is forgotten, it will wait patiently, or irritably, until it is found again. And although the paragraphs quietly submit to characteristic forces of organization, they constantly rearrange their meanings, even at the first moment you decide to think of them again. This coming and going, constant meeting and exchanging, this passionate embracing will go on and on as long as desire and will hold out, until rest, time and assimilation is again felt. Like a lover, the text is only as far away as your imagination can follow it. It is yours only as much as you struggle to be with its demands. It is the very incarnation of closeness and intimacy. And yet, paradoxically it retains its otherness, its distance, its mineral enigmatic, impervious individuality and self-containment. Like a child it leaves us even as it is joined to us, is of us, in order to exist. And frequently, hopefully, lives contentedly beyond us.

The mind and body are married, but they live in separate rooms. Even as we ignore it, reading is gathering around us like a mist, hands, like arms, like music, seducing us towards the chair, the couch, the bed. Or it finds its way hidden inside our pockets, a wrinkled piece of paper, lying forgotten in a file, or an unremembered file name.

Look how reading again draws your imagination on, towards a 'higher view.' But in that sense, as Charles Bernstein put it, 'views don't improve.' Reading is a car downtown. It gets you there and never wants to put you down. Reader and writer dance, or there is nothing. The body is suddenly, gladly drawn to its feet, turning and twisting. The words and

NICK PIOMBINO

music lead it on, through and around, around and around. A pause and then she moves about him, under him, against him, her hand, hip, his hand, hip, turn, eyes, glances, seeing and being seen, the scene, the dream, the dance, the dance, the dance.

The body, one third appetite, one third shelter, one third history.

DUNCE EMBROIDERY

show me: the reactionary imperative
linear loops and causal casualties
a significant percentage of core value

the line as irony: it works well
down a well (i.e. tidied absolution
of the mores; tempo fudge it)

fragments: the poet meant frag
(i.e. deep inside a really interesting well
scratching the walls with a pin)

you run hard you get a stitch
push then pull and make stitches
pick unpick discover palimpsest

like is there a needle small enough to
dance between what's been or just one
long lunge with a great big spear thing?

there is a world here is a word
that was then this is then
this is then too and a poem

attached replicated wisps and whispers
like: a new kind of *sermoni propriora*
in the underground skatepark

MANIFESTO

1. FIRST POSTULATE

Like a gull's egg, very light—a blink's split-second.
It's the dash that makes you human—

Here is the mouth closing—holding its portion of silence in a pearly bite—*a spark *
—a baby bird; the birth of myth. It feathers being, the flame of the games.

By which ye shall know—for the sake of things unbidden.

You learn to perform tricks with the pen—holding it loosely, *wave between finger and thumb*—that it seems to sway ((like a wand)); a willow inclined by its nature to grieve.

And you as a child desired to be buried beneath it. Then you learnt what that entailed—preferred a private baptism—

wet cross dousing, traversing the brow.

One breath's pressure on the surface of the world—a flutter 'gainst the glass.
A surge—as lucid as your dream—as though a bead of meaning trickles down the pane—using each key—to form harmonics, and sometimes, a melody.

O lean your brow against the condensation—and wait for the word.

Your jacket's fitted, nipped in at the waist—your dress is loose—so you wind a chain around the supple body—hang a clarifying gem—

It attracts lucky dust * * * the skinny prints of memory.
Magnetise it if you must—I watch you slip it into fizz * * *

Take a sip on my account.

2. INSPIRATION

Look at the pattern of matter—the spiralling shell—

((the sound of the ocean's inside you, sussurring at will))

To hold these poems in your hand—is to sleep around a soul—there's a sphere which defies explanation . . .

You're compelled to the leverage of language // anchoring itself in ink .

Then again. You hear deletion pulsing at your throat—gentle weather, enervation (we are turned like a handheld globe) and the soul spills, shivers within—

Nothing changes but the quality of nothing. Like those early evening hours—cut and fitted —and the poignancy of that. When seconds sometimes seem elastic

. . . worth a single exhalation.

There's a tenderness in each machine—like the ghost you thought you saw—like the cogs and wheels of fortune which strike out the time you wasted—

There's a tenderness in water—but en mass, it's merciless—

You write while you're visiting its edge, the ions are negative, the lesson—spraying its lace against your lips—

Gifts beneath the tree are slumped inside their boxes; are for life. The kittens live inside your skin, and play with wool—

—and hook a loop of scribble on the page.

You need to let your reader use her fingers: skirl around you, knit an intuition
** second blink ** and afterwards, a start—to blue her eyes.

As a child, you drew a row of rings—like daffy bulbs in ether white—each one the same, with the sketch of a rock on top. Futurity was on your mind, because it's something you can almost clasp—

(should another dimension allow you to fly—out of the two which form the model of a box—)

3. INFLUENCES

Wake up with a start!—who is she?

She left a well chewed toy. The sheets are crumpled by a body, might be yours.
You find tattoos upon your skin. You're puzzled, at [not so much their message, as] the script they're written in.

This one's for others, this, and this, and this—you step back, contemplate your image in the glass.

The backward lends itself to contemplation:: moves from the far out to the heart—a new
polarity: the reverse pulse of left-in text.

|/ a change is as good as a bed rest \\

while witty women writers got holed up—got plump on milk—started to scrabble at the pa-pertattered walls—

convinced a lady's trying to escape.

O cover your face—your black eyes are enough. You've learned to look at strangers as a starting point—(for love?)—although you dawdled on the day and now—it's late—

Some fellow struck the colours of the sunset. Nothing you put on the table would reveal its point of origin.

'Now you mustn't kill the general—he sets the pace for work-shy footmen. Only a hundred copies on this earth,'

The uncanny slips into itself, convinced that he's a living being—if you word it strong enough ((the tide fans out and feathers on treacherous sand))

'lest you grow weary—you grow weary—of his name.'

The light railway = tracks of phosphorous = infinite perspective in the dark.

Your vacant heart = = a bride, a simple verb == a ticket stapled to a seat—

and the ruck of its language // intermittently banded.

As the platforms flash—I think her face superimposed

—in parallax //

4. FAITH AND/IN WORK

Between believing a thing—and knowing a thing (that chiascuro of old hope)—each phoneme turns to show a profile. Holy pictures in a thumbnail.

How can you tell? They *look* like diamonds.

SARAH LAW

Roses underneath her feet.

You think the body's preservation is another act of faith—

The earth's core's origins are obscure, molten—only accessed by a cipher: the twist of graphite into itself.

It's a question of paring down: for smaller and smaller, for lesser for poorer; until the original zero postulates less than itself—

sits devoid, like a black pearl—like a black eye—

'I like to write between each assignation'
—the trudge of murder cases cakes your boots—

I start to wonder, do you think I'm looking old? It scratches away, the patina of letters—ascribing something to the sheet—and when you first hit gold, you bleed—

and when you break the pool of your skin, you weep—

a space drill—
the toughness of thin lines—
the axis of its charm kicks in—
the spinning weight between us—
like a glass lift, very bright—
and like the making of a name—
there is a danger in drawing—in drawing attention—

the aliens are out there.

These four walls allow the shields to fall to the dimensions of the page.

5. TOWARDS DEFINITION

Poetry as the sadness club? The anti-disestablishment of grief:

One small bird crashed into the glass—one limp line hanging in the hand.
The jagged edge of childhood—you never forget your first experiences; but like Byron,

you establish that much language

could twirl about the pulse.

To see you unhappy—is almost to intrude upon that mortal knowledge—which is locked until the end—which the writer, and the shrink, will whittle to a sliver.

A bundle of clothes hid in a box of tricks—the portrait and the sitter, pretty—
let's not give unwanted gifts—but only a sense of pride—

'Books have the answer': so you weave your way, in a figure of eight, to the second hand stacks.

A conversation with the dead and harried. Fingerprints of itemised leavings, all sold out within the hour—

(nothing illegal, of course)

—but bars can allocate a space—a long draft of reflection . . .

The itch propels the pearl. The ones outside the shell are malleable: keishi, lucid, sheer, and valuable.

—you'll have to wait through many curves of moon to have enough, in truth, to wrap and unwrap skeins about the wrist, and trail across a table cloth.
Leading you to me. Leading you over the edge—

A round for the captain! Eulogies for sport. 'It was a grander pastime ages gone,' but now, laureateship's confined to elegance: the royal signature—a crown with feathers in it

—and the power of the missed ship—
prisons rattling with the next in line.

Truth to tell the best investment
is the one made in your cells—

6. EDUCATION

[the ones on the back row often do well]

It's difficult to tell when framed at the whiteboard: put them in small groups and make the words work *hard*

—covert notes slipped into the arrangement—

the neophyte who makes the biggest splash;
an absent friend who's going to send it to you.

You'd think a casual approach—nevertheless, the setting up of boundaries—

No, not late again, but misinformed: the cross connections, broken links //
can leave you swinging like a Sunday bell.

I don't know how to read.

I didn't have the means to print it out, but saved it somewhere in a drive—
Friendships come and go, but your date with the muse is always a matter of trust. Or should
that be tryst.

You walked around the whole of the room before your short dance.
When once it is written, the steps get set down:

to the delicate tread of the heart—the delicate tread of the heart—

the 'mark of the teacher'—like a wound, a sashay down the corridor—
you leaf through yellow flags, and pink umbrellas, flattened by their rain.

Voice is a creaking thing—it flaps and drags itself // over formica // snuggles into leaden
windows—

is itself, defying gravity and sun.

The monk said that in death
there is a shoal we never knew
flowing through the mesh of self—

a palimpsest of whispers—
like a flock of graduands—

you are sat as guardian, motley swathing your rough cut bones.
Palms clapping down.

SARAH LAW

7. LOVES

A blessing on the psyche, and the soma, 'what you waited for'.
Nights of tapping—as though dowsing—for a stream of words—

Your hands stretch out across the table, touch the fingertips of someone.
Make the sign of the poet. Cup the air: Lift splayed fingers into slanted rain

/ ... /

Habitual creatures, writers: like the steaming mug of coffee; like the pool of light.
The Woolf at the door? A woman, at a table, writing.
Lap of voices, contrapuntal to a thought: a single whim becomes the starting spell:

the letters, the letters, wanting to read them again—

    so a breath takes shape   so a sigh shapes flesh   so an utterance
        betters the air   a loosely shifting coverlet   a softbacked spine
                    translucent in the glow of it

      you take a sip   it makes you think of things   and then forget.

          smiling just in case   it gets you nowhere

                          so a breath makes space.

A branch trembles imperceptibly; the soft snow falls.
A fence breathes, and its clutch of blue-white butterflies lift into the sky—
these shifts are the action of the hand in dream, and the body of its dreaming—

paler than you know—

I would like to write flowers into our promises.

8. READING

Implicit all along . . . the skin of a writer gets etched.

But paper is always impossible, always available: drop small coins into the well, and get you gone.

The readers recline at their desks. Their bodies levitate into the night; their books spread wings. To espouse the encoding of height—

Presents fall onto the map—soft brush of the house's mouth. She has brought you the remnants of evening, as a plaything: you plan out your course—but know that the happiest meetings are often random.

Go over the range of concentric design. She had it all drawn out, you know.

It's rare to find—but when you do, the bonds unravel—and you've a sturdy theme within your grasp—

A holding cross: the wood smooth hewn and made for liminal hours.

You've had enough of verbal consciousness. And yet a broken quote is scrolled across, and another is complete.

So I ask you. Would you let him borrow another?

Knowing that you bear an equal weight of guilt—never returning what was leant.

Printed summons—on your license—like a badly sworn-in bishop—in a spurious basilica—there's no tasteful way to say it—

but the miracles—

CODA

Cut to the trill—you've played through the concerto, and the whole thing leads to grace.

Like the lessons said, there is inquiry on the part of silence
—which you tiptoe around, and know you can sustain in friendship, being welcome and interpreted—each word a guest of the score—

a beautiful latecomer's catch / the simple frame sylphed sideways / so the light embroiders each entanglement.

ACCRETED STATEMENT (NOTES)

But I just want the effortless
mode—to sketch, scratch and
scrape idly using another layer
of attention.
But I don't want this just to be
about the self-consciousness of
writing. I want it to attempt to
inaugurate a new discourse that
flirts with and bends its strait
relations into something else.
To catch thought's pace at formed
speed (Douglas Oliver). But allow the range in:
where it is sung where it is spoken.

Poetry is the memory of language (Jacques Roubaud).

It is a question of articulation, but
as has happened so much before, the changes
can't simply be forced, I can only go on
from where I am. Witold Gombrowicz:
'The task is not to solve problems, but
only to pose them so that they attract general
attention and find their way to people. There
they will be ordered and somehow civilised'.
John Wieners as a poet of the relationship between
self and other (lover): you can talk about your
relationship and talk about the world.
Gombrowicz on Żeromski (Polish C20th interwar poet):
'Love lyricism is only superficially individual,
this state of the soul results from submitting oneself
to the species: the species inflicts violence on

a person in love and there is no significant difference
between the soldier dying for his homeland
and the lover who risks his life to possess his beloved.
Both fulfil a call that is more important
than anything personal'.

What I want is a patient acknowledgement
of immaturity. The things I assume are clear
are not necessarily. The things I assume
are simple are not necessarily. Writing against
loss of experience, memory, one's self.
Becoming what you read/write in order to understand it—
Assimilating it into your body. Writing is self.
Writing as mediating between self and world.
Writing as expression of self in world.
The dream where I was employed in censoring political
Poems by editing them. The edits actually improved
the poems but neutralised their political subtexts.
Body must become the thought or intention (Merleau-Ponty).
It's whether you feel the knowledge inside
you as part of your body—or does your sense of
self consist of other internal objects? Against
writing as simulacra, imitation of surface. Poetry
a shadow reality accentuating and counterpointing
reality—making parts of it more visible (Confucius).
The remaining ingredient is transformation.

Mini-statement (cash point advice slip):

THAT POETRY ENTERS THE BODY
AS LANGUAGE. THAT LANGUAGE

HELPS SHAPE AND FORM IDENTITY.
THAT THIS CONJUNCTION BETWEEN
BODY AND IDENTITY IS ENTRY INTO
THE POLITICAL. THAT THE POLITICAL
IS THAT WHICH RELATES INDIVIDUAL
TO INDIVIDUAL, ALWAYS ARRIVING
AT MORE THAN THE SUM
OF ITS PARTS. THE POET
AS PATTERNER OF LANGUAGE
BEYOND AND INCLUDING ITS
NORMATIVE PATTERNS OF
SUSTAINED USE EVINCES THE
TRANSFORMATION FROM BODY
INTO TEXT; IMPLICATING IDENTITY
AND POLITICS.

THE MOST EFFECTIVE MEANS OF
THIS PATTERNING CONTINUE TO BE
THOSE THAT GENERATE/ANIMATE A
TENSION WITHIN FORM-CONTENT
BETWEEN REPEATED ELEMENTS ON
VARIOUS LEVELS OF LANGUAGE:
SEMIOTIC, SEMANTIC, SYNTACTICAL,
PHONOLOGICAL, PHONETIC, MORPHEMIC.
THIS TENSION IS THE DEFINING
EMOTIONAL TONE OF BEING AS
IT STRUGGLES TO ORIENT ITSELF
IN THE FLUX BETWEEN PEOPLE AND WITHIN
ITSELF.

(Celan: 'already-no-more' versus the 'still here')

SCOTT THURSTON

Geraldine Monk:
'Poetry can be seen as a way of confronting memory in order to actively control that continuity [of memory, of self]. With poetry, language is distorted or enhanced to create new memory fields. We produce something outside our given world, so for a duration we are not observing but creating— momentarily we become the "performer" rather than the "audience".'

Poetry as dialogue between self and world—visible and invisible aspects. The veil—I knew one who lifted it (Shelley)
(the difference between being
really aware of emotions in present and the norm
of everyday life of chasing unreal things)

feelings as how we judge the significance of anything intellectual

Pound's *melopoeia*: 'inducing emotional correlations by the sound and rhythm of the speech' / form as intellectual-emotional complex

Wordsworth 'emotion recollected in tranquillity'—so can negotiate extremes of feeling

Frank O'Hara 'In Memory of My Feelings'

The resistance of the world enters my body
Feeling as a kind of thinking

Descartes describing imagination as 'simply contemplating the shape or image of a corporeal thing'

Objects contain the infinite (Claude Royet-Journaud)

HISTORY OF ART

The tree that grew through
The railing has now been cut
A lump remains: suspended

DREAM POEM

Closely they riddled
Off the Albion leading
The four deceit the bar
Seven metres my wooden
Head to knock against

Looking at old photos, the mechanical eye is
extraordinary for recording things I didn't see
—a simple snap seems to contain the secret
of the universe:

A view from a pension
Window; a patch of bare

Earth, some shrubs, a chain
Link fence, beyond things grow

In ordered rows, a gable to
The right branches spread out

Sheds to the left, a green
House, houses in the distance

but when its gaze is directed at me it feels that
there is a dangerous difference between how
it has objectified my past self *vis-à-vis* my own
memory—there is a kind of confusion
between subjectivity and objectivity which

seems to make my existence in the present dis-
turbingly arbitrary

rhyme the same in the different—carried by
sound

thinking with the things as they exist (Zukofsky)

reading other's work to get closer to my own

Gombrowicz: unmasking becomes a mask

When I hurt my knee on my first night in
Poland I didn't know what language I'd been
hurt in

To have that spontaneity, freedom to take
pleasure in creating spontaneously and use it
to bypass rational thought, but surely I need
both and at different times for different ends

'Your trouble is that you're over-educated for
your natural intelligence' (Michael Haslam) 'I
found myself dull self-protectively' (John
Wilkinson)

Defending I vs losing I
Higher sphere vs lower sphere
Honesty vs dishonesty
Unmasking vs masking (making)

SCOTT THURSTON

SCOTT THURSTON

Difficulty vs ease
Spontaneity vs persistence
Knowing vs not-knowing

Cultivating memory as civic duty (Geoffrey Hill)

How much can you discard in writing?

Keston Sutherland:
'to make the intrinsic bathos of ideas seem suddenly alien. I want poetry not to be *like* reality, but to be as impossible as reality'.

Mary Wollstonecraft: 'we reason deeply, when we forcibly feel' (but a history behind and around this statement—not easily applied to now. Keston on language as fabric of history itself.)

'Innumerable evils still remain, it is true, to afflict the humane investigator, and hurry the benevolent reformer into a labyrinth of error, who aims at destroying prejudices quickly which only time can root out, as the public opinion becomes subject to reason. An ardent affection for the human race makes enthusiastic characters eager to produce alteration in laws and governments prematurely. To render them useful and permanent, they must be the growth of each particular soil, and the grad-

ual fruit of the ripening understanding of the nation, matured by time, not forced by an unnatural fermentation.' (Wollstonecraft, *A Short Residence in Sweden*)

Wordsworth:

>   . . . a register
> Of permanent relations . . .
> manifold distinctions (difference
> Perceived in things where to the common
>   eye
> No difference is)

(Two Part Prelude ll. 341–350)

Just before, I was creating a feeling in myself of relief of the 'that wasn't so bad' order—as if recalling the feeling from memory by this trigger-statement. As I drew nearer, I felt hyper-aware of my fate, anxious of my proximity to the event in time and its inevitability as almost something I couldn't avoid, inexorably drawn toward it. I had a sensation of the future so clearly foreseen, anticipated and close, that it somehow shaded into the present: a kind of suspension. Later I saw an old man standing on Church Street, very white hair and pale face, staring open-mouthed at something—as if he was looking at a memory before him. I imagined that I might have seen a ghost of my future self, looking back at my own past.

The memory of a poem versus the poem itself —an ideal version of it—perhaps the memory of the poem before it was written

from 'Rescale':

The longest possible take possible vision
Take tenses between rush to verbal take
Between rush to plastic take on whole
Reception hold against production hold
Impose will to tame holding near role
Or far from the hold made for each
Other made for another one to hold.

∼

It doesn't hurt to play in
other fields a while for

a short heart rank shank
collects a mass at the end

whether you like it or not
—it's the hill that's all

the trick is flicking up a basket

lid of wicker racks

rather than despising every
song you sing

Intention vs non-intention
Control vs chance
Plan vs spontaneity
Reason/intelligence vs intuition
Unity/coherence vs fragmentation
Simplicity vs complexity

no remedy for all that trust (Gombrowicz)

Thinking about the issues raised negotiated by last poem (wicker basket) of language of sensual immersion vs direct communication. It specifies how to write but not what to write. However, the language of social (sic) 'sensual immersion' is directed towards the world/nature, descriptive of a response to it and descriptive of it. Also a sense in which 'nature' in the broadest sense is the place in which all intellectual problems can be solved—the world is much more complex than anything that can be written—or at any rate given representation, symbolised, metaphorised. This as opposed to the language of direct address —that which is perhaps approaching an inner reality, emotional reality—in relation to other people that gives the work an 'inside'. That both languages are in dialogue, contact, argument with each other—neither sufficient for the job on its own. I want both, I'm drawn to both. Setting up a dialectic between nature and language, outer and inner which is already false, collapsed, deconstructed (as dialectic is) but at any rate this distinction between meaning-foci of each discourse does suggest ways of continuing—reading might fuel the first and living the second—tho' a crude impossible distinction. A language of the world a language of the self. Language of the world-in-the-self; language of the self-in-the-world.

Nature—language
   | |
Reason—emotions

When I'm walking in the forest I feel constantly compelled to look back over my shoulder, register, record, fix my position, as if in slow composition of a line. But does this miss some more direct, less controlled contact with the environment?

Formlessness seeking form seeking formlessness

Earlier on walk with C—a desire to be acknowledged, watched but not negotiated with [like performing poetry?]. When walking: meditating and finding symbols for inner states (cf. Wordsworth). C otherwise introspecting without symbols—suggests two different languages (and gendered ones at that). One projects inner reality onto outer, the other reflects on inner reality. One desires silent audience, the other privacy. In the first, one disavows responsibility, in the latter responsibility is taken.

Link with maturity/immaturity: childish adult, adult child

Against the shapeless present (Miles Champion)
Caress shapeless moments (Lorna Sage)

Dream of leading someone who was blind and describing the world to her—was she also me? She was also me.

After Wieners' 'Desperation'

In what researched race, or market
the winner gives something
for what nothing defeated satisfaction?

sore loser slid
down what escape, fomenting resolution
spills lethal injection

for what lint-wrapped lover,
what short aspiration
released suitors in

hot pursuit, for the smug bust?
Vicious, hung-over, robbed
of sleep; lent divisions

unleash male violence

Poetry as a way of imagining revisiting the
dead, if not reclaiming them (Duncan Wu)

Is style something which emerges out of the
materiality of the body's emotional functions as it interacts with the sound of language?

Douglas Oliver:
'In verse organised by stress, this mental beat
which we can tap with a finger, slips through
our minds as the smallest, untrappable, experience of artistic form . . . *a notional instant
in our memory seems a present moment brimming
over with a mental content* . . . The trick makes
the *instant glide into duration* . . . thought and
emotion stand in relation to each other
rather like the instant of stress and the flow
of duration respectively. *To hit the beat most exactly, the poet follows the flow of aesthetic feeling*:
the way into the experience of the gliding instant is to live the flow most vividly, for that
is how the instant becomes filled with content,
filled with duration . . . Emotion's relation to
time or to vision . . . emotions are both recognised and interfered with by thought . . .
emotions in poetry differ from those in real
life'

Robert Creeley quoted by Norma Cole:
'Poems have always had this nature of reve-
lation for me, becoming apparently objective
manifestations of feelings and thoughts otherwise inaccessible.'

When we let the other speak we are listening
to ourselves

4th June 2003

MANIFESTOON

SHEILA E. MURPHY

Empty the self(-proclaimed) assumptive close
bought on by flocks of palace sheep

Change lanes apart from piety

Remorse, deface, unlace, replace, re-pace the
sum substantial

Deep dip lip gloss to a purer flower

Retrieve the point of living justice

Revoke the splintering of joy blend

Nominate a court case for imposing liberation

Salt the ploy demeaning flow point

Strip these pores of filth

Untie the witless drainpipe, twist it south

Lave the lake

Employ particulates to smooth inlays

Expose the hoarders

Voice a sheath of sibilants to carry rage

Endow the minuet of yore with plied noblesse

Be quaint with visitation

Camp out on the Casa Blanca lawn

Price kismet to affordable new preludes

Parse the works belonging to injurious,
enduring warlords

Dry the plates

Pertain, prevail, pre-coil

Avenge each interruption

Pry silver out of gesture

Become the beast

Bereave inflection

Mood the ring

Insult the lank

Resist your lust to fake the pass

Be relevant by default

Give latitude where none has lived

Obey prophetic regions of the skin

Be twinned, be real, be twelve

Attend to framing other centers

Fly from home toward new measures of central tendency

River the repose

Respond, revert, revere, retrace

Embellish episodes that shine not by exception

Stage a comeback from defeat and then come back

Smother counterfeit deliverance

Locate bounty

Brave the lesson plan for unencumbered violets

Name severance a short thing you'll remember

Dive into clarity and tread with calm until the shiver water talls

Find a fourth for bridging manufictive distance

Brave the heart's brain power

Pray for feast

Become the feast

Kneel to undermining sprees of narcissistic bargaining disguised as generosity

(INSTRUCTIONS)

Multi track & layer
Play with/
Play with expectation
Speak & sing
Chorus (if required)
Sotto voce (liar — and so forth)
Get them fired up
Or; you have to trick them into listening
Give everything
Spoken stage instructions
Conduction
Broadcast & blueprint
Cultures
Positive imprints

QUOTE MINE (SELECTIONS)

Writing in England is like waving the red programme of a bullfight at a menu with roast beef on it. [1]

When we're not sure, we're alive. [2]

The right ending is an open door you can't see too far out of. It can mean exactly the opposite of what you are thinking. [3]

Real art has the capacity to make us nervous. [4]

Journeys without diversion are very taxing. [5]

I'm not altogether ill at ease with boundaries. [6]

I can remember the shocks suffered by small children when they found out that at night in their own cots and under their mothers' eyes their own heads were haunted. [7]

Style is how you say what you want to say in the shortest time available, so you can all go home. [8]

If they give you lined paper to write on, write *across* the lines. [9]

A spurious reason for doing something is often a very good reason. [10]

In the rich man's house there is nowhere to spit but in his face. [11]

I don't know about you, but I practice a disorganised religion. I belong to an unholy order. We call ourselves, 'Our Lady of Perpetual Astonishment'. [12]

NOTES

1 Philip O'Connor

2 Graham Greene

3 Michael Ondaatje

4 Susan Sontag

5 W. Price Turner

6 Jenny Diski

7 Eva Svankmajerova

8 Fay Weldon

9 Russian anarchist saying

10 Will Alsop & Bruce MacLean

11 Diogenes

12 Kurt Vonnegut

AUTOMATIC MANIFESTO #9

NICK PIOMBINO

No time
no place
to stop

~

This is exactly what I remember remembering to be like, a short descriptive cue, then holding with great force to the details of one time. It is like holding on to a great tree in a tremendously powerful wind, holding on with all one's strength, why should it ever have to end?

Eventually the great wind of time will have its way and it will detach you from still another set of spellbinding specifics. How poignant these will seem from the distance of not much more than a small portion of time.

Again and again this cycle pushes and pulls me, trips me and seduces me, spinning me finally into a welter of untranslatable hieroglyphics. For a time these became fascinating almost to the point of painfulness. I can't move beyond them now. These strange, dark and enigmatic exteriors paralyzed my will. I touched them, I dissected them, I classified or should I say declassified them into a kind of prismatic system of similarities. Although sometimes in this treacherous terrain of dazzling correspondences, I strangely lost not so much my path but my will. The stimulation of foreigness at last gives way to a kind of myopic lassitude, in which the slightest combination of verbal nuances will suffice to produce a paradox so profound as to embrace contradiction. This mood, as sullen as the stormiest of winter rains, eventually, though, seems to hint of a lead to still another hidden container of embryonic residues. When finally, exhausted, I understood that the ellipse will only lead me once again to the boundary of despair, I trembled on the brink of an almost erotic affair with hesitation, doubt and procrastination!

UNMANIFEST

What the maker of a manifesto does not comprehend or acknowledge is the basic unmanifestness from which and within which each manifestation takes place. It is this neglect or ignorance that calls forth repugnance when a manifesto is proclaimed or published, especially one regarding art. As if what comes to being in and as the work of art could ever be totally manifest or even manifest at all without its abiding steadfastly in the unmanfest! A work of art is a manifesto only insofar as it is its own antimanifesto.

21 June 1983
New York

fr. Bloomsday
[Barrytown, NY: Station Hill, 1984]

THE UNIQUE ZERO MANIFESTO

Towards the Open Realism of Disclosure and a Dark-side Manifesto

A.C. EVANS

What is inevitable in a work of art is the style
— SUSAN SONTAG

What peculiar privilege has this little agitation of the brain which we call though that we must thus make it the model of the whole universe?
— DAVID HUME

Your apocalypse was fab — TORI AMOS

Welcome to **Unique Zero**—the negation of everything.

Creativity is a value-neutral process independent of all forms of expression.

Vigorously reject any notion of a generalised or theoretical 'poetic'.

The creative process is not 'theoretical'.

The specific technicalities of any art form —poetry, painting, music, sculpture, installation or assemblage—are of secondary interest, even a distraction, when trying to understand the nature of the creative process.

From the perspective of the primal creative processes there are no significant factors associated with specialised techniques derived from different artistic 'disciplines' or methods, including poetry. This is always the case, even though some media/modes/genres/forms are, in the context of overall function, or with regard to the individual temperament of the artist, more suited to purpose than others, de-pending upon viewpoint. Furthermore, distinctions between 'non representation' and 'abstraction' are invalid: all artworks are, in the first instance, symbolic representations or constructed reifications, even 'found objects', 'ready-mades' or 'conceptual' artefacts. Nevertheless, a 'symbol' can also be non-figurative (non-objective) and can be described, loosely, as 'abstract'.

All artworks derive from the personality, the mentality, of the *auteur*. They are polysemic/polyvalent, symbolic objects having as their primary raison d'être the externalisation, via signification, of the psychological-onto-logical, infinitely evolving presence/existence of the *auteur* (author/artist/poet) without whom the 'work' (*opus*) would not exist and without whom language is meaningless.

THE CULTURAL MILIEU

This process of externalisation (trace or trail) takes place within a specific socio-cultural context (or *Zeitgeist*) that partially shapes the final outcome. It is possible to 'transcend' the socio-cultural context, although it very difficult to do so. The chronotope in the cultural 'ecosystem' locates the *auteur* (poet/artist) in a socio-cultural milieu or contextual *mise-en-scène*, based on the enforcement of norms within specific social structures such as the class system, caste systems and the means of economic production.

Normative structures, sustained by ideology and belief (*participation mystique*) are usually experienced as hegemonic and repressive to some degree. Such normative structures are Blake's 'mind-forg'd manacles' of cultural oppression and structural evil and must be psychologically accommodated through sublimation, the discharge of instinctual energies into non-instinctual, ideologically sanctioned forms of behaviour. A form of false consciousness tending toward narcosis is a by-product of this sublimation mechanism.

On the other hand, the normative ideology ('culture') of any social system is also capable of the infinite assimilation of any artefact, however innovative, progressive, recondite, radical, marginal, outrageous or avant-garde. In advanced economies any artefact will also be the inevitable subject of homogenised commodification by the forces of The Market. Cultural oppression works through all those inhibiting, regressive, ideological normalisation effects persistently degrading the chronotope, both locally and globally (law of entropy) in the interest of various authoritarian cultural-spiritual power elites. Such high caste power elites may declare war upon 'false gods' and each other, but they are all united by an imperative to criminalize the imagination; alongside dope-fiends, loose women, idolaters and apostates, free thinkers and artists—makers of 'graven images'—are the real enemy.

The 'Open Realism' of the unrestrained imagination, a mode of extreme naturalism encompassing the antinomian syzygy phenomenon of complementarity, works against this perpetual state of dispossession, and works for the nullification of everything; a Unique Zero opposed to the wretched standing joke of rigidified 'culture'. The unreality of the chronotope ensnares the subject in an infinitely receding hall of distorting mirrors where the conflict between utilitarian austerity and indulgent individualism cannot be recognised as a smoke screen. In this context, artworks can be either transgressive or conformist, although the poetic process is innately transgressive (non-conformist) because all art can induce a de-familiarisation (disclosure) effect perturbing, however weakly, the hegemony of the mainstream and disrupting the inauthentic discourse of 'idle chatter' (they call it 'metaphysics').

Even if ultimately inconsequential, even if only an imperceptible 'shudder' (*frisson nouveau*), a perturbation of the chronotope and its normative, cultural signifying systems is a transgression—and all such perturbations or disturbances are taboo. But the 'purpose' of the poem/work is exploration and discovery at the edge of zone; to explore the experience of limits, to explore experience off-limits; to discover or probe the borders of the human event horizon; to actualise singularity, the aporetic neither-nor and/or both.

However, the transgressive or conformist nature of any given artwork will also depend upon the worldview (*Weltenschauung*) of the *auteur*/poet. The dynamic, dialectical interplay of *Weltenschauung* and *Zeitgeist* at a singular point of intersection (*auteur*-nexus) within the chronotope influences the subject's sense of identity, even though the chronotope may exist in a perpetual state of flux or emergence (the rigidity of cultural norms notwithstanding). The poetic process itself is a problematic factor with regard to the question of identity and can enter into a state of conflict with the ideological basis of the prevailing *Zeitgeist*. The subject's personal *Weltenschauung* may, in reality, be a form of false consciousness—bad faith, 'structural evil', *meconnaissance* or *avidya*. Interpellation, the mechanism of economic and cultural assimilation, may create an unstable atmospheric 'I' (a 'they-self' or mirage persona) that is not the same as the subject's 'true (real or empirical) self'. Most artefacts are determined by the phantom signature of this 'mirage persona', rather than the authentic signature of the artist's true will, Sontag's 'principle of decision'.

These factors impact upon attempts to define an individual style, poetic or authorial 'voice' or *maniera*. Assertions of authorship *per se* can be compromised if it appears that personal identity is 'nothing but' a projection, an ideological/socio-economic 'construct' of mass consumer culture, the product of an all-pervasive theocratic hegemony like so-called 'higher' culture bedevilled by the self-serving Aristotelean humbug of 'virtue' and 'magnificence'. Alternatively, the mirage persona is often confused with, or can masquerade as, the vulnerable and immature empirical self. Yet, the inauthentic, fragmentary they-self can never be the 'real' *auteur*.

INWARDNESS AND 'POEISIS'

'Inspiration' and 'talent' are conventional terms denoting certain mental capabilities and imaginative capacities. Imaginative activity (active imagination) is 'driven' by innate obsessions or fixations with atavistic affinities, possibly of genetic origin. This compulsion, or impulse, finds 'expression' in an exploratory immersion process of 'inwardness' or descent (the dangerous passage, the voyage to the interior, the night sea journey, the quest or anti-quest).

The 'descent' or 'inverse pilgrimage' (*katabasis*) is fraught with anxiety, obstacles and difficulties. This experience assumes the character of an ordeal—an ascesis, even—realised through 'rites of passage' comprising three known stages: separation—initiation—return. During this process the subject will encounter or confront uncanny horrors and paranoid connections. These terrors may include resurgent atavisms (the phylogenetic inheritance), pathological forces, every form of self-violation (*mortificatio*) and shadowy, chthonic 'elementals'—all characterised by a ubiquitous undertow of archaic nostalgia. The subject is exposed to all the underworld horrors of personal and collective unconscious contents (the 'inferno') and other phantasmagoria—such as tutelary 'threshold guardians'—derived, in the final analysis, from psychic formations known as 'archetypes'.

These 'archetypes' (collective representations or 'categories') can be either structures or paradigmatic processes, not just primordial images. Archetypes are not immutable, and naturally-occurring changes at the archetypal level (creation, evolution, decay, extinction) are reflected by corresponding changes in the prevailing *Zeitgeist* or world order. Phenomena such as cultural implosion, drift, lag, paradigm-mutation and belief-system burn-out (the death of god, the death of art) manifest themselves through collective

time/'deep' history (*Geschichte*) just as pain is 'referred' away from an injured site to various other parts of the body. Thus, 'archetypes' can, and do, mutate over time. The archetypal level is, naturally, inherently unstable and without foundation.

Phantasmal figures and motifs (the inchoate raw material or *massa confusa*) arise from a dynamic, unconscious process driven by libido or unbound psychic energy. This inwardness or immersion process discloses the centre of desire (the heart of darkness, the end of the night, the final frontier), a duplicitous 'inner world' (inner space) of cosmic cruelty, proto-animistic fetishism, polymorphous perversity, illicit propensities, unrestrained fantasy, iambic scurrility, primal narcissism, pathological fixations, retrogression and antinomian 'otherness'. Creativity involves both assimilation of this dark-side (the mutant spectres of desire) and psychic de-conditioning (deconstruction) from the effects of cultural-ideological interpellation (belief, 'spirituality' and 'metaphysics'). Deconditioning is achieved by immersion in darkness (blackening or *noircissement*) or, alternatively, by passage through the dark, haunted depths of the 'enchanted forest', the legendary wild-wood.

The 'heart of darkness', the capricious, macabre and sinister 'dark-side', and its shadowy, subconscious strata of involuntary memory (personal/collective) is the first level of the subject's inner core, an emergent feature of mutable, fluidic, psychic topography derived from the semiotic, proto-symbolic chora (*la chora semiotique*). However, the phantasmal 'contents' of the dark-side derive from both 'inner' and 'outer' experience: the products of indefinite feedback, everything but the soul. Characterised by the paradoxical, perceptual complementarity of syzygy phenomena (chaos/cosmos, causal/a-causal, subject/object, latent/manifest, light/dark, positive/negative, life/death, psyche/soma, masculine/feminine, self/not-self, fact/fiction, true/false, love/hate, demotic/hieratic, signifier/signified, wave/particle, etc.) the 'contents' reflect the indeterminate, bipolar, existential structure of the 'real'. This is the case, even if there can be no such 'thing' as Reality, realism being a quality of understanding.

A primal phenomenon, not sensible or intelligible in itself, the *chora semiotique* is the universal pre-linguistic precursor 'matrix realm' (the Platonic 'receptacle of becoming', the *unus mundus*, the quantum vacuum, the *anima mundi*, the abyssal depths) which underpins all symbolism, language and meaning. It is beyond rational understanding, merging with the 'sympathetic' autonomic nervous system and the primeval (visceral) sphere of the 'old brain', that proto-sentient, pre-logical 'reptilian' and limbic armature of the unconscious anatomy. Creativity consists of a non-verbal, irrational, intuitive, instinctual procedure of imaginative 'shaping/forming' or 'making' (*poeisis*) utilising the subject's entire psyche—although internal incoherence and psychic division always inhibits optimal creative functioning and free plasticity. Phantasmal contents are subjected to a pre-logical transmutation process (*khemeia*) comprising condensation (metaphor) and displacement (metonymy), articulated through the osmotic interchange of free association (automatism), energised by libido (*vis creativa*), predicated by differentiation and conditioned by 'objective chance'.

This process generates a first phase 'work', *opus*, or artefact, shaped by the gratuitous laws of organic form (deep form) showing how reification becomes representation through metamorphosis. These representations generate, at the level of reader or audience response, an inter-subjective experience, effect or simulation, of 'significance', 'meaning' and aesthetic 'value' and, almost instantaneously, are co-opted or annexed as vectors of cultural interpellation.

INVENTION AND AESTHETIC EFFECTS

Primal *poeisis* functions independently of all self-conscious artifice, taste, thematic concerns, genre conventions and artistic method, although form and technique can be conventionalised at the socio-cultural level and always are. Naturally the *auteur* (poet/artist) will also work self-consciously, simultaneously exercising intellectual ability (*ingegno*), wit, erudition, virtuosity and acquired capability in the utilisation of all facets of creative technique both ancient and modern, formal and informal: style, structure, and content. Yet, the fortuitous automatism, the non-verbal visuality of primal *poeisis* will, at all times, suffuse every aspect of the work in hand, including the objective technical factors mentioned.

However the faculty of invention (*invenzione*), comprising discovery, representation and all modes of reification and transformation (inflections, modifications, recapitulations, transpositions, modulations and permutations), is rooted in the automatic mechanism of the libidinous process.

In its pure state (*l'art pour l'art*), poetic invention operates surrealistically (*sans sujet préconçu*) upon, and within, the psyche. It draws an intuitive, elemental 'spark' (*scintilla*) from the encounter between, and/or juxtaposition of, mutually exclusive or distant realities: 'kitchen-cynic' naturalism colliding with mythic symbolism, for example, or a weird fusion of pastoral Arcadia and urban inferno.

Invention can draw the same elemental spark from the off-beat, marvellous-uncanny 'inbetweenness' properties of 'alien', interstitial phenomena; from an erratic oscillation between the trite and original, or historicism and futurism; from an incongruous synthesis of low-tone and grand manner or from an irregular union of preciosity and brutalism. Often tragicomic, sometimes bitter-sweet, invention can endow the ephemeral with gravitas, transmuting the despised and the neglected into high art or high camp, into an underground freak-out (ufo) precipitating a mind-warp (*dérèglement de tous les sens*).

The process may manifest in different rhapsodic 'poetic' lyrical, or, alternatively, 'anti-poetic', passionless non-lyrical, modalities. Modalities such as melopoeia ('phonetic' or 'musical') or phanopoeia ('visual' or 'pictorial') commingle with complimentary modes of functioning such as *pathopoeia* (working with affective elements such as feeling, mood and emotion, even with estrangement, irony and alienation) or mythopoeia (Euhemerism/mythologisation/mythic parallelism).

The epistemological element of 'meaning' (semantic relations, etymology, associations, nuance, denotation and connotation) endows

A.C. EVANS

the artefact with communicative properties and linguistic capacities that engage with consciousness and psychosomatic exteriority, acquiring in the process a patina of 'cultural value'.

Meanwhile, at the level of the chronotope, the subject interacts impressionistically with 'the world' via an interface conditioned by the multidimensional, dialectical interaction of sensation, *Zeitgeist* and *Weltenschauung*. Here, through a dialectical interplay of material forces, events and subjective perceptions (e.g. synchronicity and coincidence), inspirational feedback (friction/irritability) continues to fuel and inform the poetic process on a mundane day-to-day basis. This magic-circumstantial aesthetic redemption of banality enhances intensity of perception and poetic intuition, even if it does not necessarily effect a diminution of existential unease, anxiety or 'angst'.

To some degree this entire procedure is 'convulsive' (explosive-fixed) insofar as it arises from an energetic spasm, a surreal analogue to geological seismic activity, triggered by ritualistic intercession, in alliance with the pleasure principle. This 'nervous spasm' is the climax or consummation (*Chymische Hochzeit*) of the initial impulse. The degree of convulsive intensity generated by the primary processes is conditioned by the level of intensity inherent in any given creative act or event and also depends on the neurological or mental state and personality of the *auteur*.

This intensity is manifest as an emotional spark or charge comprising energy quanta of attraction/repulsion energising the artefact at an extremely deep level within its infrastructure. In a specifically poetic context the affective/emotional charge, or *cathexis*, invests the imagistic, lexical and other structural elements of a work with a quantum of aesthetic 'power', either weak or strong.

The charge will have an enigmatic 'effect' (*la sorcellerie évocatoire*), even, perhaps, an absurd effect of hilarity—provoked, for instance, by cynicism, burlesque, iambic parody, black humour or the vitriol of corrosive satire—upon both the reader and the writer. This outcome can be heightened in certain cases to the level of a paranormal 'numinous effect' (uncanny intensity of feeling) that is often misrepresented in mystical terms by both poets and readers. This problem arises, for example, in apocalyptic or 'vatic' (visionary) art and is often associated with the transcendental view that all art aspires to 'the condition of music'.

The degree of charge/intensity also determines the transgressive potential of the work on the socio-cultural plane. Furthermore, the exact nature of the 'uncanny' effect (*das*

Unheimlich) and/or response in specific instances is infinitely variable, multi-factorial, unpredictable, hallucinatory and indeterminate in conformance with The Uncertainty Principle. Audience or reader-response will be conditioned by, among other factors, individual predisposition, immediate circumstances, state of health, degree of socio-cultural alienation, collective expectations or inhibiting horizons demarcating the phobic, ideological miasma of false consciousness.

PARAPRAXIS

The open-real 'lifted horizon' (epiphany) of de-familiarisation is a consequence of disruption (perturbation or infraction) of the *auteur*-nexus within the chronotope and, correspondingly, within the psyche. This inter-penetration of the inner and outer worlds of the reader-writer causes a parapraxis or subversive breakdown of normality; a shamanistic 'breakthough in plane' (a vector, rupture, tear, wound or gateway) disclosing 'alterity' (aporia, otherness, surreality, hyper-reality, super-reality, the dis-placed and the dis-located) warping contingent historicity, displacing the distorting mirrors of the hyper-culture.

Alterity, in this context, may be defined as the bizarre (or 'convulsive') antithesis of false consciousness which embodies the manifest unreality of the prevailing socio-cultural hegemony. De-familiarisation may generate a heterodox mode of 'open realism' (disclosure, desacralization) in contradiction to the oppressive unreality (narcosis) of the phenomena of false consciousness and specious 'identity'(national identity, social identity, cultural identity). Such phantasmal, collective, consensual mirages of interpellation maintain social and psychological control through denial of the self, ultimately inducing ideological de-realisation (etherealization or dissolution) in the vapours of mystical unreality euphemistically called The Cloud of Unknowing.

Yet, faced with the impossibility of 'saying' anything 'new', creativity takes its revenge, ruthlessly recycling, plundering or pillaging the phenomenal, theatrical, kaleidoscopic 'spectacle' of the world for 'raw material'. From a position of 'absolute divergence', creativity enhances the autonomous potential of the spontaneous, singular, side-real imagination in a perverse, even tawdry, spirit of panache; a spirit of intransigent opposition, a 'negative dialectic' of contradiction and reverse exegesis, working, always, against the grain, subversively 'against nature' (*contra naturam*). To reduce the eternal to the transient, to transform substance into style, the 'signature of the artist's will'—that is the essence of modernity with its 'art-house' experimentalism, with its 'cool' cosmopolitan, radical chic, is it not?

Within the chronotope, the falsehood of the subject's specular mirage persona may be compromised or exposed by aesthetic manipulation of double images, wordplay, rhetorical devices and figures of all kinds including 'multiple personalities', alter egos, authorial 'voices', poetic 'masks' and heteronyms. Similarly the integrity of the poetic process can be jeopardised by self-division and psychic fragmentation. From this perspective 'impersonality', or aesthetic distance, is simply one mask among many, just one survival strategy among others equally valid or invalid.

No strategy can be guaranteed, not even Nihilism, Stoicism or Epicureanism. Not even the decadent, dandified insouciance of cultivated dilettantism. Not even the daunting complexities of Post-modern theory—not even the ironies of high camp; not even the mass media *glitzkrieg*. No, not even the free-floating aestheticism of marginal dispossessed 'outsiders' inhabiting 'unseen' paraxial, liminal regions of cultural and sub-cultural life.

The creative process has two outcomes: first, an impact at the socio-cultural level, and second, a psychoactive (psychotropic) effect within the psyche of the individual subject.

This 'psycho-activity', this psychedelic epiphany, is an end in itself and the motive for the original creative fixation-compulsion (impetus/impulse). Through feedback this fixation-compulsion evolves into a process of developmental integration, a process of growth-change through 'altered states' of lucidity or 'systematic derangement' (*raisonné dérèglement*), defined as 'individuation'.

Often misrepresented in 'spiritual' terms and thus neutralised, or blocked, by false consciousness and the devious contents of the mystical mirror-world menagerie or cultural hothouse, individuation is simply the human manifestation of a general drive to entelechy (autarchic self-realisation) common to all living organisms, one aspect of the parabolic arc of the evolutionary process. Artistic activity, as a mode of ontogenic-phylogenic self-actualisation, has an evolutionary function (survival value, realisation of singularity) at the biological, species level.

Enrichment of the anguished existential spectacle; enhanced adaptive capacities; the 'pataphysical subversion of interpellation in the name of an 'impossible', absurd freedom (*la liberté absurde*); intensification of the contemporaneous, perceptual 'now' (the inadvertent lucidity of the 'sublime moment', the gem-like flames of synaesthesia); the infinite, ambivalent reinvention of modernity. These are some possible benefits derived from creativity. Others might include the cathartic purgation of 'spiritual' accretions, blockages and restrictions impeding psychic integration. However the autonomous imagination is indifferent to such 'benefits' and, being neither benign nor malign, its ultimate effect may well be 'off-centre', may well induce disarray and further confusion: a sardonic 'debacle of the intellect'.

The reification and externalisation of the artwork, its conformance to expectations within objective, historical parameters of social exchange, art or anti-art fashions, styles, schools, genres and movements in the fragmentary world of the mirage persona or they-self, is a by-product of this natural process. Nevertheless the *opus* or 'work' may have important, quasi-autonomous cultural effects and implications. These implications are acute when viewed against the background of inevitable, infinite and eternal psycho-aesthetic warfare occurring within the social theatre of the chronotope—the perpetual sectarian conflict and generational revolt between successive schools of thought and ideological movements within the hegemonic domain of cultural oppression. These conflicts, transfigured and intensified by the underlying struggle (*agon*) between the palliative unreality of false consciousness (inauthenticity) and the paradoxical symbolic-naturalistic 'open realism' of disclosure, will never end.

Expanding and transforming the shared cognitive-epistemological-ontological framework, testing the cultural event horizon, in accord with the arbitrary and 'uncanny' principle of 'strangeness' and the characteristic 'charm' of the unexpected, The Work creates its own tremors and aftershocks, its own future—and the nullification of everything.

A wilfully sibylline world is speaking through the gaps in a henceforth unviable reality
—ANTONIN ARTAUD

Exeunt omnes.

Frisson nouveau—HUGO
Noircissement—CÉLINE
Sans sujet préconçu—BRETON
Dérèglement de tous les sens / raisonné dérèglement—RIMBAUD
La sorcellerie évocatoire—BAUDELAIRE
La liberté absurde—CAMUS

TO ALL YOU SQUABBLING POETS

For everything you've ever said, or thought to do, the road take your eye!

May you lie under perpetual malediction, bored to death by the monotonous logic of chanting nuns.

May you aim ceaselessly towards your featureless targets; be lost forever in an interminable fog, like flies trapped inside ping-pong balls.

May you be buried in a midden of bird bones & soup ladles, ignored by archaeologists, forgotten by all.

May you always be the lonely poker player, detached and confident, doomed to lose.

May you ride your lurching sled over the fantails of snowdrifts, no home in sight, no point to give you bearings.

May life remain as puzzling today
as when you first discovered it.

No. Let everything be explained to you, leaving nothing to imagination or learning.

May you take small comfort in your memories.

Let your only company be a team of depressed angels trapped in the past.

O that your mouths be plugged with wads of grass as you lie for centuries beneath the surface in a bed of schist.

Go! Head to sea in an offshore wind.

Spend years adrift among the frozen cracks.

We are bored with all your ballyhoo & noise!

You are the reason we turned off.

TO ALL THE USELESS IDIOTS IN THE FUTURE

I hardly know where to start but now I have
please note that I am by no means a sad
and utter joke far from it one sunny day
I will astound the passers-by and cause
even birds to fall from the sky you may
laugh but notice please how clothes and
other goods dropping in price means that
poor people can look well fed and casual
not just tattered backdrops to Cathy come
Home no wonder they bombed the fuck out
of us such chaos and filth underfoot so many
bad haircuts and worse armpits thank God
the history books don't give us the smells
so tell us how we can stop all these illegals
like Artaud I am convinced there have been
gatherings of Mexicans lamas and rabbis
to weaken me by masturbating collectively and
plan to retaliate by leading a party of fifty friends
armed with machine guns to invade Tibet
crawling up their beaches onto meadows
that's why we have doors and windows I
am oh so very tired of dialogue and reason
still the same control only the controllers got to
feel better about themselves despite that they
decide what gets written and who can write maybe
this pithy piece will fit in a bottle then bob along in the
lovely briny and get washed ashore some happy century
to be read like Bukharin was by cleaner minds and
in the shining air I will emerge and reclaim mine.

THE CERTAINTIES OF MANIFEST POEMS

NATHAN THOMPSON

#1

'freedom is'
to forget to account for
all of your possessions
a robbery of sorts
under rubber tulips

#2

discussion might be appropriate
'is that my navel'
a lop-sided tree
indicates the direction of south
if I forgot how to navigate
would you still love me

#3

the skeletons are coming
how they move is a mystery
'the mechanics are really very simple'
you left your car here
what was I supposed to do
the keys are in the ignition
that's right   we're everywhere

#4

the celestial highways have opened
roads to here are nothing to speak of
once you're there the turnaround is predicated
'a sequence of numbers pattering in a bag'
cross-reference the dreams that things are made of
extending our tentacles in the dark
this much is certain   something articulate
pulls out on the near side

NATHAN THOMPSON

ACKNOWLEDGEMENTS

Terrible Work for David Bircumshaw's 'Ghost Machine Self-Assembly Kit'.

EastWesterly Review and *Postmodern Village* for Lael Ewy's 'Towards a Manifesto for New Poetry'.

The Rules (Poor Tom's Press) for Brian Fewster's 'The Rules'.

Scintilla for Rose Flint's 'City of Cherished Words' which also won second prize in the *Scintilla* Poetry Competition 2005.

Neon Highway and *Great Works* for Mark Goodwin's 'La belle Dame Sans Matrix'.

Forklift.Ohio for Bob Hicock's 'Troubadour'.

Parthenon West Review for Janis Butler Holm's 'Bother'.

The Word Hoard for an earlier version of Keith Jafrate's 'manifesto'.

The *Poetics* list and *RIF/T* for Ira Lightman's 'Manifesto (1995)'.

Ribot, *Boundary 2*, *Crayon* and *Theoretical Objects* (Green Integer) for Nick Piombino's 'Automatic Manifestoes'.

Raw Edge Magazine for Dave Reeves' 'The Raw Edge Blues'.

Scratch for Guy Russell's 'Manifesto of the Self-Publicists'.

Roxy (West House Books) for Gavin Selerie's '*Roxy*: Section 34'.

The Anti-Orpheus: A Notebook (Shearsman e-book) for a version of Robert Sheppard's 'A Voice Without', and *New Writing* for 'Not Another Poem'.

Stride for Paul Sutton's 'To all the useless idiots in the future'.

Otoliths for Andrew Taylor's 'A Poetics of Absence'.

Oulipoems (Ahadada) for Philip Terry's 'Advice to a Young Writer'.

Staple for Scott Thurston's 'Accreted Statement'.

CONTRIBUTORS' NOTES

DAVID BIRCUMSHAW is a proxy Warwickshire lad from the decayed beauties of inner city 1960s Birmingham who now lives in walking distance of the dead in King Lear's citadel Leicester. Books include the impossible to find in print *Painting Without Numbers* and *The Animal Subsides* (Arrowhead, 2004). Edited the online and maybe to be revived *A Chide's Alphabet* (2001-3). E-books include *Parousia* (2004) and *The Cabinet of Dr Spectare* (2008).

A.C. EVANS lives in West London. A regular contributor to *Stride*, *Fire*, *The Supplement*, *Midnight Street*, *Inclement* and *Neon Highway* among other magazines, A C Evans works in the tradition of the bizarre and the grotesque but defines his work as realist. Influenced by Romanticism, Decadence, Aestheticism, the iconoclasm of Dada, revolutionary Surrealism and the immediacy of Pop, he regards these as points of departure, none as a destination —we live in a post avant-garde world. Poetry, he claims, is an infinite quest for self-discovery and an inevitable indictment of both established dogmas and the prevailing *radical chic* orthodoxy.

ANDY BROWN is Director of Creative Writing at the University of Exeter. His two most recent books of poems for Salt Publications are *Fall of the Rebel Angels: Poems 1996–2006*, and

Goose Music (co-authored with John Burnside). He trained as an Ecologist, a discipline that informs his poetry and criticism which appears in *The Salt Companion to Lee Harwood*. He has been a Centre Director for the Arvon Foundation, and is a recording and live musician.

LAEL EWY's work has appeared in *EastWesterly Review, Santa Barbara Review, New Orleans Review, Writer's Bloc, Denver Quarterly, Chelsea, Mikokosmos, Wichita City Paper* (as a columnist*),* and *Naked City*. He is currently on faculty at Hesston College and Wichita State University and is the co-founder and an editor of *EastWesterly Review*, an online journal of literary satire at www.postmodernvillage.com. He enjoys busting his knuckles on an old Volvo and an even older Mustang and making sand mandalas with dynamite.

BRIAN FEWSTER was born in Nottingham and studied English at Cambridge. After spending two years on VSO in India, he taught for 25 years but changed career with an MSc in Computing from De Montfort University and worked as an IT administrator and technical author, spending part of each week in London. His poetry has won several prizes and been published in *Poetry Review, Envoi, Orbis* and elsewhere. His most recent publication is *Sym-*

pathetic Magic. His other main interest is politics and he was the Green Party's lead candidate for the East Midlands in the 2004 European election. His poems are consequently often informed with a satirical bite. His voice was silenced in June by a stroke subsequent to cancer.

PETER FINCH is a literary agent, a poet, a performer and a psychogeographer. His work is best read in *Antibodies* (Stride), *The Welsh Poems* (Shearsman) and, most recently, *Selected Later Poems* (Seren). His prose work is in *Real Cardiff* (3 vols) and *Real Wales*, all published by Seren. He was once a publisher, has been a bookseller and currently runs Academi, the literature promotion agency for Wales.

MARK GOODWIN received an East Midlands Arts Writers' Bursary in 1996, and An Eric Gregory Award in 1998. He has published widely on paper and online. Mark writes in various styles, and revels in exploring ways words play. Some of his work expresses 'pastoral' concerns; some of his play could be described as cartoon-esque mischief; later poetry utilises various procedures, particularly 'gapping'—where spaces are inserted to rearrange rhythm and create multiple syntaxes. Mark lives in Leicestershire where he works as a community poet. *Else*, his first full-length collection, was published by Shearsman in May 2008.

KEITH HACKWOOD lives in Newport, South Wales, where he also works as a counsellor and psychotherapist. He has two books of poetry currently in print—*Charon's Hammer* and *One Hundred Sonnets Of Galactic Love,* both published by PS Avalon.

ALAN HALSEY's work appears in two substantial selections, *Marginalien* (Five Seasons 2005) and *Not Everything Remotely* (Salt 2006). A new collection, *Term as in Aftermath*, was recently published by Ahadada.

DAVID HART, born in Aberystwyth, lives in Birmingham, has been (many years ago) a university chaplain, theatre critic and arts administrator, and now lives as a poet, with recent part time teaching posts at Warwick and Birmingham Universities; residencies include psychiatric and general hospitals and Worcester Cathedral, was Birmingham Poet Laureate 1997–98; books include *Setting the poem to words, Crag Inspector* and *Running Out* (Five Seasons Press 2006).

BOB HICOK's most recent collection, *This Clumsy Living*, was awarded the Bobbitt Prize from the Library of Congress. His other books are *Insomnia Diary* (Pitt, 2004), *Animal Soul* (Invisible Cities Press, 2001),a finalist for the National Book Critics Circle Award, *Plus Shipping* (BOA, 1998), and *The Legend of Light* (University of Wisconsin, 1995), which received the Felix Pollak Prize in Poetry and was named a 1997 ALA Booklist Notable Book of the Year. A recipient of three Pushcart Prizes, Guggenheim and NEA Fellowships, his poetry has been selected for inclusion in four volumes of Best American Poetry.

JANIS BUTLER HOLM lives in Athens, Ohio, where she has served as Associate Editor for *Wide Angle*, the film journal. Her essays, stories, poems, and performance pieces have appeared in small-press, national, and international magazines. Her plays have been produced in the USA, Canada, and England.

KEITH JAFRATE is a poet and musician whose most recent collection was *Songs for Eurydice* from Stride and whose latest CD, *when bill danced the war*, a collaboration with Canadian writer Sarah Murphy and sonic artist Shaun Blezard, was issued by The Word Hoard. He's part of the text-music collective orfeo 5, who have just released their first CD *a year on the ice*, as well as being a member of The Word Hoard, an artists' co-operative based in Halifax.

LUKE KENNARD is a poet and writer of fiction. His previous collections are *The Solex Brothers* and *The Harbour Beyond the Movie*, which was shortlisted for the Forward Prize for Best Collection, 2007. He lectures at the University of Birmingham.

MICHAEL KERR began his adult life as an entrepreneur but, after developing a near-fatal aversion to numbers, he returned to school to follow a passion for writing. His poems and creative nonfiction have appeared in *Prick of the Spindle,* a chapbook of poetry entitled *Luggage Trunk of Air Hostesses,* and various other publications. He was the winner of the 2007-08 Herman Schmeling Award for Expository Writing at Southern Oregon University and his work has been nominated for inclusion in *The Best Creative Nonfiction, Vol. 3* published by W.W. Norton. He lives in Ashland, Oregon.

SARAH LAW is a senior lecturer in creative writing at London Metropolitan University. Her published collections of poetry are *Bliss Tangle* (Stride, 1999), *The Lady Chapel* (Stride, 2004) and *Perihelion* (Shearsman, 2006). She is interested in medieval mystics, contemporary innovative poetry, and many things in between.

Since 1995, IRA LIGHTMAN has put himself forward for the Anglican ministry, and been rejected; then moved into the art world and radio, where he makes Public Art and cartoons for Radio 3's *The Verb*. He works extensively with mathematics, and patterns, often inventing forms for communities to make work in. For Radio 3, he celebrated the 300th anniversary of Pi, and the 450th anniversary of the Equals Sign with Peter Finch. His first book available from Shearsman. He lives in North East England and has two children. More at www.iralightman.com.

RUPERT LOYDELL is Senior Lecturer in English with Creative Writing at University College Falmouth and the editor of *Stride* magazine. From 1982-2008 he was the Managing Editor of Stride Publications, a wide-ranging and hyperactive small press. His solo poetry collections include *Boombox*, *An Experiment in Navigation*, *Ex Catalogue*, *The Smallest Deaths* and *A Conference of Voices*; he has also published collaborative works with Peter Dent, Robert Garlitz, David Kennedy, Sheila E. Murphy, Robert Sheppard and Nathan Thompson .

STEPHEN C. MIDDLETON has had several books of poetry published, most recently *Worlds of Pain / Shades of Grace* (Poetry Salzburg) and *A Brave Light* (Stride). He has featured in five anthologies, including *The Stumbling Dance* (Stride) and *Paging Doctor Jazz* (Shoestring). He was editor of *Ostinato*, a jazz and jazz related poetry magazine, and The Tenormen Press, producing limited edition illustrated books of music related poetry. His live work includes readings, storytelling, performance pieces with musicians, and stand up comedy. He is currently working on a project (prose and poetry) involving jazz, blues, politics, folk art, mountain environments, performance ethos, and long-term illness.

MICHAEL MOLYNEUX is a philosophy graduate from Preston who works as an Educational Support worker and, out of term time, a painter and decorator. His main influences are Wallace Stevens and Pablo Neruda and his new collection *The Ballad of the Night Wind* is scheduled for publication in autumn 2008.

ANDREA MOORHEAD was born in 1947 in Buffalo, New York. She is editor of *Osiris* and author of several collections of poems, including *From a Grove of Aspen* (University of Salzburg Press), *le vert est fragile* and *Présence de la terre* (Écrits des Forges). She is a member of ALTA (American Literary Translators Association) and has published translations of contemporary francophone poetry in Canada and Germany. She teaches French at Deerfield

Academy where she is Director of the Deerfield Academy Press.

SHEILA E. MURPHY is a widely published poet. Stride Publications brought out several of her books. Forthcoming from blue lion books is her *Collected Chapbooks* and from Luna Bisonte Prods a selection of visual poetry in collaboration with K.S. Ernst. Murphy lives in Phoenix, AZ, USA.

MARIO PETRUCCI is an ecologist and physicist, the only poet to have been resident at the Imperial War Museum and BBC Radio 3. He is four times winner of the London Writers competition, inaugural pamphlet selector for the PBS, and a Royal Literary Fund Fellow. *Flowers of Sulphur* (Enitharmon, 2007) received an ACE Writers' Award and a New London Writers Award, while his Arvon-winning *Heavy Water: a poem for Chernobyl* (Enitharmon, 2004) was made into an internationally acclaimed film (Seventh Art Productions). Described as 'Heartfelt, ambitious and alive' (*Daily Telegraph*), Petrucci has been credited with creating 'Poetry on a geological scale . . . a new track for poets of witness' (*Verse*). The poems printed here are from his radical new sequence *i tulips*, due from Enitharmon in 2010.

NICK PIOMBINO opened his ongoing weblog *fait accompli* in February, 2003. His books include *Poems* (Sun and Moon), *The Boundary of Blur* (Roof), *Light Street* (Zasterle), *Theoretical Objects* (Green Integer), *Two Essays* (Leave), *The Boundary of Theory* (Cuneiform), *Hegelian Honeymoon* (Chax). *fait accompli* (Factory School), *Free Fall,* (Otoliths), and *Contradicta,* (Green integer), with collages by Toni Simon. Anthologies include: *The L=A=N=G=U=A=G=E Book*, *In The American Tree*, *The Politics of Poetic Form*, *From The Other Side of the Century*, *The Gertrude Stein Awards in Innovative American Poetry*, *Close Listening*, *Manifesto: A Century of Isms* and *E-X-C-H-A-N-G-E V-A-L-U-E-S, the first XI Interviews*.

KYRILL POTAPOV is twenty. He is an undergraduate at the University of Kent studying English and Creative Writing. He has written a number of short stories (including 'Death of the Cat', the counterpart to his manifesto) and is working on his second novel. His play *Hitman: A Response to Fear and Loathing* was produced and performed in The Venue, University of Kent in the spring of 2008. He is unpublished.

DAVE REEVES is a writer, performer and blues musician. He edited and published new writing journal *Raw Edge Magazine* for 13 years, distributing 16,000 copies per issue, free at the point of collection. Currently touring poetry and spoken word with self-accompaniment on bluesharp and squeezebox as 'The Wooden Horse of Dr Troy' and with multi-instrumentalist Tom Cook as 'The Whirled Service', he also organises Extreme Writing Workshops at various literary festivals. He is now a partner in the online spoken word radio station www.radiowildfire.com appearing as a presenter on their live transmissions.

GUY RUSSELL was born in 1965 in Chatham and currently works as a Business Analyst for the Open University in Milton Keynes. Recent publications include poems in *The Interpreter's House* and a story in *Brace: A New Generation in Fiction* (Comma Press). Reviews sometimes in *Tears in the Fence*.

GAVIN SELERIE was born in London, where he still lives. He was formerly a lecturer at Birkbeck College. His books include *Azimuth* (Binnacle Press, 1984), *Roxy* (West House Books, 1996), *Days of '49* [with Alan Halsey] (West House Books, 1999) and *Le Fanu's Ghost* (Five Seasons Press, 2006). He has appeared in anthologies such as *The New British Poetry* (Paladin, 1988), *Other: British & Irish Poetry since 1970* (Wesleyan University Press, 1999) and *The Reality Street Book of Sonnets* (RSE, 2008). *Music's*

Duel: New and Selected Poems 1972–2008 is due from Shearsman Books in 2009.

ROBERT SHEPPARD has recently published his poetry in his long project *Complete Twentieth Century Blues* (Salt 2008), and in *Hymns to the God in which my Typewriter Believes* (Stride, 2006). *Warrant Error* is forthcoming (Shearsman). Also a critic, he has published *Iain Sinclair* (2007) and the edited volume *The Salt Companion to Lee Harwood* (Salt, 2007). A theorist, practitioner and pedagogue of the speculative discourse of poetics, he is Professor of Poetry and Poetics at Edge Hill University. He lives in Liverpool and edits the blogzine *Pages* at www.robertsheppard.blogspot.com. and co-edits *The Journal of Innovative British and Irish Poetry*.

GEOFF STEVENS has edited and published *Purple Patch* poetry magazine since 1976. His poetry has been published widely and often in Europe, America,and Australasia. His latest books are *Absinthe On Your Icecream*, and *Previously Unpublished Selected, Poems 1975-2007*. He regularily performs at poetry readings.

PAUL SUTTON was born in London in 1964 but brought up in Hertfordshire and Wiltshire. He studied at Oxford (Jesus), worked in industry, left to travel, and now teaches English at a secondary school. The contrasting joys and rages this produces are exactly the inspirations needed for writing—especially the actual reception given to supposedly popular mainstream and 'multicultural' poetry. A related inspiration is the liberal elite's attempted stranglehold on poetry and literature —the dishonest control and moral guardianship (over language and much else) they seek. He sees prose poetry as a way of exploring and subverting this power grab.

ANDREW TAYLOR is a Liverpool-based poet and co-editor of *erbacce* and erbacce-press. His latest collection *And the Weary Are at Rest* is published by Sunnyoutside, Buffalo, New York. He recently completed a PhD in Poetry and Poetics.

PAUL TAYLOR is a musician, working worldwide with Columbian maestro Roberto Pla's Latin Ensemble, Snowboy & The Latin Section, and many other bands. He has developed a unique solo project, trombone poetry, which interweaves spontaneous music and poetry at literary and music festivals and clubs. The CD, "Speech", is available via trombonepoetry.com His interests range from evolutionary theory to Oulipo to the designs and visions of Buckminster Fuller.

PHILIP TERRY is the author of *Ovid Metamorphosed* (2000), *Fables of Aesop* (2006),and *Oulipoems* (2006). His translation of Raymond Queneau's *Elementary Morality* was recently published by Carcanet. He is currently Director of Creative Writing at the University of Essex.

NATHAN THOMPSON grew up in Cornwall and studied at the University of Exeter, where he later lectured part-time in musicology. He now lives in Jersey. *the arboretum towards the beginning*, his first collection, was published by Shearsman. A chapbook, *A Haunting*, will be published by Skald in 2009.

SCOTT THURSTON's most recent book is *Momentum* (Shearsman, 2008). He edits *The Radiator*, a journal of poetics, and edited *The Salt Companion to Geraldine Monk*. Scott lectures at the University of Salford and has published widely on innovative poetry. See his pages at www.archiveofthenow.com/.

ANGELA TOPPING is the author of three poetry collections, two with Stride, and the most recent, *The Way We Came*, with bluechrome. She has also edited two anthologies and her work has appeared in numerous books including children's anthologies. She also writes critical books for Greenwich Exchange, with one published last year and two more in the pipeline. She is married with two daughters and has been teaching English since 1989, firstly in FE, then secondary schools. Writing and teaching are her main passions, aside of a love of music and nature.

STEVEN WALING is. He has been 50 years and will hopefully continue to be for some time. He has published: *Calling Myself On The Phone* (Smith/Doorstop) and *Travelator* (Salt). Poems continue to fly about everywhere as he continues to write them, in magazines, and online. He has just escaped from being a Writer-in-Prison, and is now on the run to his next book. His blog is: www.stevenwaling.blog spot.com

CLIFF YATES was born in Birmingham. He teaches at Maharishi School and works as a writer and creative writing tutor. His debut collection *Henry's Clock* (Smith/Doorstop) won both the Aldeburgh First Collection Prize and the Poetry Business Book & Pamphlet Competition. He wrote *Jumpstart Poetry in the Secondary School* during his time as Poetry Society poet-in-residence. His latest pamphlet is *Emergency Rations*. He received an Arts Council England Writer's Award for the poems in his latest collection, *Frank Freeman's Dancing School* (Salt).